SUPERVISION CAN BE EASY!

SUPERVISION CAN BE EASY!

David K. Lindo

A Division of American Management Associations

Library of Congress Cataloging in Publication Data

Lindo, David K   1936–
  Supervision can be easy!

  Includes index.
  1. Supervision of employees.   I. Title.
HF5549.L494   658.3'02   79-17682
ISBN 0-8144-5548-4

First Printing

Preface

Supervision can be easy but seldom is. Why is that? Because the tremendous array of problems, people, laws, policies, and procedures a supervisor is expected to handle is constantly increasing. When you become a supervisor, the general subject of supervision quickly becomes specific and personal.

Supervision is more than telling a subordinate what to do. The complete supervisor is a coach, teacher, disciplinarian, producer, communicator, and often friend. Although many supervisors recognize their importance, they are extremely uncomfortable in these roles. The tools presented in this book will help supervisors develop the skills they need to make the job more comfortable.

Starting as a supervisor is difficult. But by striving to get to know the people involved, both your boss and your subordinates, you can improve your effectiveness. I was terrified when I accepted my first challenge as a rookie supervisor. A college degree and one year of on-the-job experience didn't prepare me for instant success in my new role. And no tools were offered to me either. Formal supervisory training came later—after many an unpleasant emotional crisis. Twenty years of trial and error, failure and success, helped me develop a number of simple, easy-to-use, effective supervisory tools. These are identified and illustrated in this book in a showcase of on-the-job applications.

This book is not a technical discussion of theoretical concepts. It is a practical, easy-to-read guide that includes many tips about how to handle supervisory concerns and problems. I've identified five areas that seem to give most supervisors trouble. Supervisors (new or experienced) can improve their performance by investing effort to solve these problems. The five areas correspond to the five major parts of this book.

Part I, on supervisory style, provides a foundation for the supervisor to learn more about himself and how he relates to his work group. It identifies actions that must be taken to stretch his span of interest and perfect a span of control.

Part II, which focuses on communications, provides the framework of techniques the supervisor needs to sell ideas, communicate goals, establish productivity, and build a cohesive work group.

Part III examines evaluation techniques—ways to zero in on individual performance and then appropriately recognize and reward it. It also includes pointers on when and where to find subordinate staff.

Part IV focuses on control responsibilities, reminding the supervisor that a significant aspect of the job is developing good personal work habits. This part identifies the need to stretch the workday, practice good financial control, and achieve performance objectives.

Part V, on career planning, is intended to help the supervisor measure his present and evaluate his future. By applying the principles presented, the supervisor can promote himself and actively plan and encourage subordinate promotability—thus creating an environment for career growth.

Supervision is one of the most underrated jobs in the employment community. Whether a person is a second-shift foreman, a supervisor of government records, or a skilled technician in charge of engineers or accountants, he will be faced with a demanding and challenging workforce—and an array of laws and situations that defy description. Supervisors must be ready to accept a variety of challenges. And they must succeed. Strong middle management is vital to the success of any firm.

This book and its illustrations are designed to start the new supervisor off on the right foot. In addition, the book will help the old pro perfect and polish his or her techniques. Although many of the examples emphasize managing an administrative, white collar segment of the workforce, the principles discussed have broad application. They work equally well in factory, engineering, accounting, legal, clerical, and sales environments.

David K. Lindo

Contents

PART I
Be More Than You Are

1

Bigger Job: Stride Out

Congratulations. You are a supervisor. The person who takes all the credit for good—and blames someone else for everything that's wrong. Does it really work that way? No, it doesn't. As a supervisor, you've just taken a job that requires more work than ever. Perhaps this is a well-planned step in your career program. In that case, you've got ideas and a future agenda ready to go. But what if the promotion comes as a total surprise? What if you've been named supervisor before you're ready? It may be a big break or a big bust, and it may be happening to you right now. Developing a program to manage unexpected opportunities can help you turn them into big career breaks. Believe it or not, you can create a plan that generates success.

If a promotion comes as a surprise to you, the news may stun other supervisors and shock your subordinates as well. What do you do now? Establishing rapport *must* be your first objective. The most important aspect of managing is not technical expertise. That certainly helps, but working with people is what the job is all about. If you delay establishing a close rapport with subordinates in your new supervisory role, you will soon lose the chance to develop it.

A valuable approach to start with is to hold one-on-one staff interviews. You must plan ahead to make them work for you. Keep in mind that your objective is to establish that vital rapport early. The interview involves the use of a number of documents prepared in advance, as the following section shows.

GET-ACQUAINTED INTERVIEWS

Interviewing job applicants is common; interviewing "old" employees is not. Set up a schedule to talk to each of your subordinates individually—and stick to it. Get acquainted: learn to associate a face with a name. Give people a chance to meet you too. Hold the interview on neutral ground—not in your office or theirs. This is an informal get-acquainted interview, so sit on the same side of the table or desk as the subordinate. In this way you indicate you are on his or her side—and the subordinate can easily share your notes.

In preparation for these 30-to-45-minute sessions, you should draw up a list of your current performance standards and job objectives and release it to your people. A general list is given below. (You should add specific statements to suit your needs.)

PERFORMANCE STANDARDS
1. Follow work rules.
2. Maintain a positive mental attitude.
3. Establish meaningful, measurable objectives.
4. Complete tasks by due dates.
5. Set appropriate priorities.

JOB OBJECTIVES
1. Give the boss on-time, on-target performance.
2. Keep current on developments in my area of responsibility.
3. Maintain technical competence.
4. Apply appropriate supervisory techniques.

Whenever possible have the previous supervisor prepare a position importance evaluation (PIE) form on each employee. (See Figure 1-1.) If you cannot obtain this data from the previous supervisor, other sources include: your boss, supervisors in work-related departments, or "customers" of your department's output. By noting how frequently people perform tasks for others and objectively rating the importance of these assignments too, you can easily identify the key department members.

Figure 1-1 is from an accounting department. With modification it will also work for engineering, personnel, sales, and other departments. Higher point totals indicate people with higher job value. The completed form also indicates specific duties performed, whom they are performed for, and the frequency of that performance.

The next step in preparing for the interview is to ask each employee to fill out a staff interview record. (See Figure 1-2.) The data obtained from this form offer an excellent starting point for the interview. Again, if the example doesn't fit your situation, you should prepare your own questions. Try to get your employees to tell you what they think, what they like, what they've tried, what they do, and so on.

Another important preparatory step is to obtain the employee's personnel file (if one exists). Personnel files tell interesting stories, but they can be misleading. Seldom will they give you any indication of what capabilities or interests an employee has. Comments by other managers on the employee's accomplishments, strengths, and experiences are at best vague, at worst unfair. However, look for trends in performance, education, and work habits. These may identify severe problems that must be solved early. Here are examples that I have found.

One fellow was upset because he'd been promoted to an exempt job without really having a choice. The promotion cost him money: His pay raise was well below the overtime pay he had been receiving as a nonexempt employee. To top it off, he worked longer hours, only now the overtime was uncompensated. In another case a supervisor gave a low rating to a man because he had been missing assignment dates. The man's workload was nearly double that of the employee sitting next to him. Yet the neighbor received a higher rating.

Job descriptions are part of the personnel files of exempt employees. These descriptions are evolutionary. Periodically up-

Figure 1-1.

Position Importance Evaluation Form

The supervisor is to fill out the form opposite for each employee. The form should be completed in the following steps and returned before the get-acquainted interview.

	STEP	EXAMPLE

1. Select from the left column work which this employee performs.

      1. Issues an audit report once a month.

2. Determine the left-most recipient of that work.

      2. A director and two supervisors receive the report. Therefore, the director is the left-most recipient.

3. Determine the number of points applicable to that work from the rating scale provided.

      3. This person would receive 8 points, since he issues a report to a director each month.

4. Repeat steps 1-3 for all the employee responsibilities listed. If any are missing, write them in.

5. Total all points on the matrix.

Employee

Recipient

Communications Issued or Prepared	Customer	Director	Manager	Supervisor	Administrator	Interdepartmental	Other
Operations analyses							
Audit reports							
Cost reviews							
Situation summaries							
Cost control reports — nonroutine							
Work orders and authorizations							
Routine repetitive reports							
Research reports							
Procedures statements							
Presentation handouts							
Cost catalogs							
Memoranda							
Teaching or training							
Data base maintenance							
Other (specify)							
Total points							

Rating Scale

Often — at least once a week	20	16	10	8	6	4	4
Regularly — at least once a month	14	8	5	4	3	2	2
Infrequently — less than once a month	10	6	4	3	2	1	1

Figure 1-2.

Staff Interview Record

Employee _____ Date_____

Career path objectives:

Recent educational development:

Items best liked about position. Why?

Items least liked about position. Why?

Items most important to position. Why?

Most critical department problems:

Hobbies and interests:

What suggestions, improvements, or new ideas have you made within the past year? Have they been accepted or rejected? Do you know why?

What direct contact with the top two levels of management have you had in the past three months? What were the subjects discussed?

Discuss in detail the following items related to your assignments and responsibilities.
(a) Where do source data come from?

(b) What is the timing and frequency of these data?

(c) Do you maintain a log of incoming data?

(d) What do you do with the information when you get it?

(e) When you are finished with the data, who gets your output report?

(f) How much of your job is manual? How much of the information is mechanically generated?

What new reports or assignments have been added to your workload in the past year? Who requested those items and why?

Which reports previously prepared by you have been dropped in the past year? Why?

Who is your backup? Can he or she fill in for you in your absence?

date them with each change in job content. Even though they may be obsolete as written, they can help you measure progress. A routine annual update aids communication and adds to your understanding of what each person is doing.

After you assemble and study all this material, create a set of interview notes for each employee (See Figure 1-3.) This saves valuable time in the actual interview. On the form you can add key items that are discussed during the interview. In the interview it's easy to take the lead and review data with each person. You can explain how people can put money in their pockets by helping their supervisor obtain the "right" results—from which you can "write" a good merit review.

During the interview, stress the following elements:

1. Position duties.
2. Accomplishments.
3. Job objectives.
4. Continuing-education programs (even self-study).
5. Your desire to help the employee meet or beat his or her goals.
6. Employee strengths.

As a side benefit, you should try to find:

1. Employees' expectations of you.
2. Interests shared by the group that you can sponsor or that you must reverse.
3. Ways to identify with members of the group.
4. Irritations that may exist between members of the group, between your department and others, or between employees and you.
5. Philosophical differences. Here you may find that high-priority jobs are done as time is available rather than as needed and that employees take work direction from a lot of people other than you.
6. Employee preparedness. Do employees bring a pad of

Figure 1-3.

Interview Notes

Employee _____ Company Start Date _____ Today's Date_____

Current position (grade)_____

Latest performance rating   1__ 2__ 3__ 4(Top)__ Date_____

Previous performance rating   1__ 2__ 3__ 4(Top)__ Date_____

Previous performance rating   1__ 2__ 3__ 4(Top)__ Date_____

Degree_____ Degree year_____

Latest noted educational entry (and date, if given):

Experience:

   Years with company _____

   Years in department_____

   Years in current position (grade) _____

Status of professional staff data sheet: Current____ Needs update____

Bring a pad? Yes____ No____

Assignment completed? Yes____ No____

Strengths _____

_____

Weaknesses_____

_____

Items discussed during interview:_____

_____

Actions to be taken based on interview:

By supervisor: _____

_____

By employee:_____

_____

paper along? Did they expect you to say anything of importance? In advance of the interviews you can hand out a noncritical assignment to test the mood of the group. Did the employee do it? To your satisfaction?

7. Backup people and plans for their future development.
8. Existing departmental problems (to help you identify needs for change).
9. Informal departmental leaders.

The interview is also an excellent opportunity to relieve the employee's fears. You can do this by noncritically listening to him and allaying his concern about where he stands with you. You should restate your goals and evaluate their effect on the employee. Tell him the content of his personnel file and discuss the salary review program, telling him what he can do to score best. Review your notes with the employee and point out how he fits into the department. Believe it or not, many people with three, four, or more years of experience won't know. Finally, you should answer any questions the employee has.

Vary the style of your interview to suit the needs of exempt professionals, bargaining units (unions), and clerical personnel. Make clear that you stress equal employment opportunity.

Through the first 30 days make few changes. Study, question, evaluate, and learn. You may make changes in minor items—for example, rearranging seating to alleviate noise or space problems. If the work duties identified are beyond the scope of the department's current name, change it to become more descriptive. Later, using the information and experience you have gained, you may make more affirmative changes.

The results of this program—a quick start and identification with your people—will pay dividends as long as you have your new position and may convince your superiors that you're just the person to take over an even higher job in the future.

2
Find Your Supervisory Style

As you step into your supervisory job, you probably will already know everyone in the department and their duties. An immediate problem is how to establish supervisory distance—to demonstrate that you are no longer "one of the boys (or girls)." You can delegate duties because you feel confident that you could fill in on most of the jobs. You have little fear that a job will go undone if someone fails.

If you successfully make the transition to supervisor, you will qualify for further promotion. Next time, the changes required will be greater. You will have to know and apply more than the elementary principles of supervision. You will spend more of your time on organizational problems. Don't wait. Now is the time to concentrate on broadening your methods of communication and sharpening your language skills.

Replacing the supervisor of an existing department can be difficult. Many factors are involved in taking over a new group. For example:

1. You don't personally know the people. All you have is a personnel file.
2. You must supervise people whose duties you don't know.
3. You need to learn duties from the top down instead of the bottom up.

4. You are more visible to management.
5. A higher-level job brings increased pressure.
6. Decision making is further away from the detail knowledge.
7. The job has a quicker tempo.
8. You must increase delegation of duties.
9. You must give courtesy and consideration to more people.
10. You need broader support.
11. You may face competition for the job from a subordinate.
12. You bring your previous reputation with you. How you rate on fairness, honesty, and experience will precede you. And the ratings may be distorted.

If the department's previous supervisor had a style different from yours, your leadership problem becomes greater. Meet the challenge positively. Can you find any benefits to the old leader's style? Do you *need* to adjust? How much? Decide if you must make a sudden or a gradual change. Ask yourself, "Why do I do what I do?" The answers will help you determine the style that's right for you. But what is style?

A supervisor's speech and actions reveal his spirit, his habits, his capacities, his biases. Blended together, they describe his management style. Style is that distinctive mode of behavior you have developed to deal with superiors, peers, and subordinates. A distinct style, once established, becomes a habit that is hard to change. And it becomes a supervisor's trademark.

YOUR CURRENT STYLE

What is your current management style? How do others perceive it? Perhaps you've been described as fair, honest, hardworking, reasonable, flexible. There are as many appropriate management styles as there are supervisors. But like a suit, each must be tailored to the wearer to be at its best. Shop around for some alterations. Practice changes. Recognize the necessity to vary your style throughout your career. Don't be afraid to modify something that doesn't feel right to you. Actually, each new position you take or subordinate you deal with offers an opportunity to redefine your style.

Do any of the following statements describe your management approach today?

"He always adjusts himself to others. Gets the most possible from available material. Invents variations to existing formations, much like a good coach adjusting to the double wing T. Gives everyone a voice in developing objectives. Acts, but only after obtaining available input."

"He forces others to adjust to him. Issues objectives, rules, opinions, and guidelines like a new coach installing a split T offense among players experienced in the single wing."

"He both adjusts to others and has them adjust to him. Uses the split T and tries to draft and train his personnel."

Your style is broadly based on your experience, temperament, education, ability, patience, and the time constraints you face. To help define your style, answer these questions:

1. Are you vocationally, educationally, and mentally prepared to be a supervisor? Or do you prefer to do each task yourself?
2. What kind of training did you get from previous managers?
3. Are you a problem seeker or a problem solver? (Some people find only problems in every opportunity to change or grow.)
4. How much overt status, prestige, and power do you have? How much do you think you need?
5. What is or was your manager's style?
6. What is your opinion of departmental personnel? Of departmental goals? Are they adequate?
7. How much retraining do incumbent personnel require?
8. Do you like a lot of managerial distance or a little? (How

close in salary to subordinates are you? Does this bother you?)
9. Do you apply sophisticated supervisory techniques, including interviewing, evaluation, work direction, and objective fact-finding?
10. Is your reputation based on your ability with people or production? Are you known as a hatchet man, a fire fighter, a problem avoider?

As you answer, beware of projection. Don't automatically assume that others will see you as you see yourself. Selecting the right style for your current job depends on your answers to the questions. (The style that worked for you in your last job will not be a perfect fit today.) Thus the "right" style is elusive, and it will change.

YOUR CURRENT DEPARTMENT

If you have been with your firm for any length of time, you already have a reputation and a style. It may be overstated, understated, misunderstood, or something else. Take time to test your words and expressions. Are your standards on salary increases, meetings, schedules, formats, personnel, and support requirements similar to those of other departments?

Relate your management style to your subordinates' working styles. People work for themselves, but they will accept direction from you. Find out their expectations. The best way to do this is to listen to them. Schedule some discussion time. Open communication can eliminate or at least define style conflicts. Give people a chance to identify how to work together to improve the environment of the department. Here is a checklist that can help you review your efforts. Did you:

1. Get acquainted with each subordinate?
2. Review personnel files?
3. Discover and allay fears of employees?

4. Obtain current job descriptions and position objectives for each?
5. Establish a communication path to cover crisis situations?
6. Spend time listening to people and encouraging expression of their views?
7. Obtain agreement on job standards?
8. Find out what people like and dislike about your style?
9. Develop team working commitments?
10. Demonstrate your real interest in your subordinates?

Motivation and creativity are positive environmental forces, but they are not automatic. If they are crushed by the weight of restrictive supervisory styles, there is little chance that they will magically appear at higher levels.

Is your current style appropriate for each supervisory situation? In working to develop an appropriate style, you should communicate in a way that comes naturally to you. Then improve on it. Join a writers' club or a speakers' group. Make sure you work from suitable objectives. Clear them with your boss and communicate them to your subordinates. Always be sincere in your dealings with people. And, most important, put yourself in the background and learn to listen.

Do not overlook the expert information available at your local library. You don't even need a library card. Just do some research and then select from the best ideas available. Also create contacts with local universities, hobby groups, and other organizations. Comparison with other departments and people can be helpful too.

What is your management style? Is it working for you? Could it be better? Should you change it? If you decide to change, set priorities. Establish a time schedule and create the management style that works for you. Using an appropriate style will help you gain the acceptance of your subordinates, help your group perform up to potential, and put you in line for further promotion.

3

Advance Yourself and Others

To really feel comfortable as supervisor you must be confident of your ability to supervise. Your confidence level can be quickly tested. How do you answer the following questions?

Do you feel you've really completed the big step up to supervisor? You haven't completed that step until you make a positive move toward the next job. Although on the surface everything seems serene, now is the time to start growing out of your current job. Does that thought give you a queasy feeling in your stomach?

Do you wonder what the people you've already passed over are thinking? Is your supervisory world filled with doubts? Do you worry that at any moment a subordinate may come to you and say, "You lucky so-and-so. What do I have to do to get promoted? Why did you get that job? How can I grow? What are you going to do to make me promotable? Tell me your secret."

These questions are nearly impossible to answer if you're still new in your job. Even a seasoned supervisor can have trouble satisfying them. Keep in mind that not everyone will be promoted. There is only one spot at the top. Nevertheless, you must

Adapted, by permission of the publisher, from *Supervision,* a publication of the National Research Bureau, Inc. © November 1976.

keep new and former colleagues working hard—for themselves, for the department, and for you.

A supervisor must spend time and effort helping those with potential to develop. Many supervisors don't. How do you show your interest to a subordinate, young or old, who says, "This job is pointless, I want to do something else. Where am I and where am I going?"

Recently I heard a young man from an accounting department complain, "I don't have a real job. Nothing I do is significant. But I don't know what to do about it. Should I quit—or is it the same everywhere?" In response to the suggestion that he discuss his feelings with his supervisor, he exclaimed, "But I tried that! He just said my work was important. I asked him what else I could do. He had no answer. When I asked why, he got defensive and said, 'I'm busy, go back and do your work.' "

Contrast this with a supervisor's reaction to the complaints of a 20-year veteran employee. Apparently the man's salary had topped out, his future was behind him, and he was faced with the specter of inflation, increasing family expenses, and no more salary increases. He was uncertain and unhappy. He felt that he had to stay where he was. "How can I change jobs at 45?" was his lament. He hadn't thought that it would be even more difficult at 48 or 50. His supervisor heard the cry of frustration, involved the personnel department, and helped him find a new job—a new lease on life.

What common supervisory problems do these two people present? Do both have time and opportunity to prepare themselves for the status you've achieved? As a supervisor, you have an obligation to constructively help subordinates grow, whatever their age or experience.

HANDLING REQUESTS FOR ADVANCEMENT

One of the most difficult aspects of supervision is to decide when an incumbent employee expects you to offer him a "better" deal than his old supervisor gave. This is especially difficult if you are new to the department. Should you take the position that the employee is totally responsible for developing himself? What is a bona fide request for advancement?

There are several approaches you can use. To start the conversation rolling, you can ask, "Can you specify the work you want and tell me how it relates to your abilities?" The sincere person will be able to give you an answer. It is important to clarify this point early. Why? Because you may not have the kind of work available that the employee wants. If you don't, you may have to suggest that he look elsewhere to match his talents and targets. Good employees are hard to find. And it is expensive to recruit and train them. Switching a "good" employee to another department within your firm can be cost effective.

Other supervisors may not believe you when you tell them that your employee can do their job. However, if they have an opportunity to see the employee demonstrate his ability, they will be more likely to accept your recommendation. Force employees to take assignments that give them visibility. Help them practice for their next job. Take some time to prepare a list of problems that other departments face. Allow subordinates to practice solving as many of these problems as your schedule (and that of the other departments) permits. Do this in conjunction with the other department. Avoid misunderstandings that may come about if someone interprets your action as a takeover attempt.

If you do find a match for one of your employees in another department, the timing of the job opening may still be a problem. In this case you may have to channel the employee into a corollary position or "parking orbit" for a few months. But this time doesn't have to be wasted. Waiting time can be aggressively used for training or task-force or special assignments—or for a well-earned vacation.

One developmental experience is fighting for your employees. Support and defend them when they make mistakes, use the experience as a coaching aid, then repeat the process. Don't expect instant success. Any new task will involve mistakes. If the potential error is a costly one, do the job in parallel so you can quickly shift to the alternative method or person.

Another factor you can identify in subordinates is their willingness to invest in their own future. A secretary in an electronics firm uses every extra minute she can find to complete an educational program that will gain her an administrative post. She does her secretarial duties as quickly and efficiently as possible, then works on developing new skills (unrelated to the secretarial post). By not wasting moments in idle chit-chat, she hastens the day when she will get the job she wants. And she's proving that she's a valuable and productive employee to her firm.

BUILDING CAREER PATHS

If you cannot move a deserving person ahead now, you can still discuss and resolve other items of concern. Begin by getting the subordinate's definition of "ahead." The individual must identify where he is in relation to where he wants to go. You can help by listing all the checkpoints you feel are significant to his progress. It is helpful to keep a scorecard or developmental record. (See Figure 3-1.) Point out to your subordinate that the items on this record must be periodically updated.

I've asked employees to describe what motivates them on both work-related and non-work-related activities. Then I've had them categorize each motivator in relation to their current job and their target job. Some surprising answers have turned up. It's not unusual to find people in the wrong field, the wrong job, or the wrong career. Their motivation and their work aren't the same. Thus they "don't like their job." Yet they are locked in place because they see no alternatives. You can help them find new jobs that complement their interests.

In addition, remind subordinates that they can ask family, coworkers, friends, educators, even the personnel department,

Figure 3-1.

Employee's Developmental Scorecard

	What I Want	Obstacles	New Skills Added	How Did I Do?	Objectives Accomplished
From Work					
3 years ago	____	____	____	____	____
1 year ago	____	____	____	____	____
Now	____	____	____	____	____
1 year from now	____	____	____	____	____
3 years from now	____	____	____	____	____
Away from Work					
3 years ago	____	____	____	____	____
1 year ago	____	____	____	____	____
Now	____	____	____	____	____
1 year from now	____	____	____	____	____
3 years from now	____	____	____	____	____

What will I do this year? Who can help me? _____

"What do you think I enjoy?" Each can play a key role in generating a list of "enjoy" items. These in turn can be used to define the person's target job—his "what to do" objective.

Analysis of where the employee is now is a valuable starting point. The next step is to create a career growth path to connect these two points. Bear in mind that the ability of the individual could be a limiting factor to upward growth. Thus for some people "ahead" may be lateral growth. Give the employee assignments that test his abilities. He is more likely to believe that he lacks ability if he discovers it for himself than if you merely tell him he doesn't measure up.

The next step in moving an employee ahead is making an "investment decision"—often a major obstacle on the path. How much time, money, and effort can you, the company, and the employee give? I've found that many success-oriented people can't handle this aspect of growth. Depending on the employee's objective, becoming a "success" may mean laying out money to entertain sponsors, pay tuition, join clubs, or add books to a personal library. A suitable wardrobe and polished personal appearance can be a drain on employee funds. Time taken away from family, friends, recreation, and hobbies is also a real sacrifice. And political interrelationships must be developed. These often require personality adjustments. Identify the price tag for the employee. Be candid.

On the other hand, perhaps promotion in your firm is not related to clubs, books, or wardrobe. Does the brown bagger have as good a chance for promotion as the country clubber? Will going to the Saturday picnic with his wife and kids instead of sharing the experience of cutting budgets with you help or hinder his chances? Be very honest with subordinates on how you and your firm view vital areas.

You can point out that commitment to advancement also requires learning new skills and solving new problems. But make sure that advanced education will really help the employee move ahead in your company. I've heard managers insist that a subordinate obtain a degree. They exclaim, "It will really help you. It's a key part of your development program. Get your degree and you can really go places.'' Yet when the employee gets the degree, there is no appreciable change in job or salary. As a result, the employee learns: (1) the principles necessary to earn a degree, and (2) not to believe his boss. Such an employee will go places—generally up the street to the competition.

Once the employee has acquired sufficient technical skills, he must be given the chance to apply them. Without immediate application learning is soon lost, and frustration replaces it. To sustain learning, you must delegate new problems to the employee, even on jobs you feel are critical. This is an end in itself. By solving these problems, the employee is increasing his competence. Don't worry about him taking your job; instead, help him aspire to it. To enhance his aspirations, encourage him to read job-related periodicals. They can provide new ideas for application. Continuing formal or informal education adds new strengths too.

The final and perhaps most difficult step on this path is to get your subordinates to make a firm commitment. People are reluctant to say their goals out loud. They find it even more difficult to put them in writing. Yet simply voicing a goal—saying ''I want Job X'' or ''I am ready for Job X''—enhances the commitment to achievement. Once you hear an employee make such an assertion, open up. Sincerely listen to the subordinate's proposal. Discuss it with him. Let him know you will be seriously involved in helping him achieve his goal. This includes finding a replacement, then helping the employee develop.

Insist that your organization take advantage of every opportunity to profit from the abilities of your subordinates. And if you really can't help, say so. Explain your reasons. Why? Because if the worst happens and the right job doesn't materialize, you know you did your part and your subordinates will too. If you help your subordinates grow, you will be recognized too. You get the credit for a strong department. And *you* can't move ahead without an adequate replacement. Work hard for your employees. The payoff is feeling comfortable as a supervisor. The next step depends on you.

4

Separations Are Never Easy

Perhaps the most difficult, emotion-laden supervisory duty is ending an employment relationship with a subordinate. There are four general categories of employment separation:

Leave of absence
Transfer
Layoff
Termination (voluntary and involuntary)

Each of these, handled properly, can reduce the strain on the employee and you. They present unique opportunities for you to develop and display needed human relations skills—including patience, understanding, and communication. It is worthwhile to spend some time preparing yourself for each form of potential staff turnover.

LEAVE OF ABSENCE

Perhaps the easiest form of turnover to handle is the subordinate-requested leave of absence. You probably expect this to be routine. After all, what can go wrong? The subordinate leaves on a specified date for a specified reason—military ser-

Adapted, by permission of the publisher, from *Supervision,* a publication of the National Research Bureau, Inc. © May 1975.

vice, pregnancy, illness, or some other pressing personal reason. The employee returns at a predetermined date. Unless policy does not exist or is not followed, approving the leave is normal. Still, problems can occur. Before you nod your head, read your personnel policy very carefully, and coordinate your statements and actions with the personnel department. If your firm doesn't have a policy, talk to the personnel director. Doing so may help you avoid problems.

One supervisor's secretary requested maternity leave. She clearly stated, in accordance with company policy, that she expected to return to work. The department had a heavy typing load, and the supervisor needed skilled secretarial help. Unfortunately, unaware of his company's policy, he hired a replacement, a full-time secretary. He did not tell her the job was over when the woman on leave returned and demanded her old job back—as was her right.

The supervisor now had two secretaries. Although he preferred the replacement, who was a more productive employee, he was forced to reinstate his first secretary. His bias toward No. 2 affected work assignments. Result: Bad feelings from No. 1. She filed a complaint. The local human rights commission stepped in. The supervisor spent many sleepless nights and nearly lost his job before the smoke cleared. Policy was met. Both women were reassigned. The supervisor got an education in state and federal regulations too. The moral? As supervisor, be sure you understand and can objectively apply company personnel policies and current legal regulations.

TRANSFER

Transfers can be used to acquire or get rid of subordinates. Bear in mind that after a transfer the employee remains with the company. If you hurt feelings or make an enemy, the employee will still be around.

A poorly handled transfer can have long-ranging effects. For example, if the employee was marginal and you "sold" the receiving department on his or her qualities, your judgment will eventually be questioned. Do it often enough and you'll earn a reputation as a poor judge of people, a developer of marginal employees, or something worse. Marginal employees should not be transferred unless you have determined that they are misplaced in their current job. It's no service to your firm or to employees to periodically move them around the company. It increases costs and merely shifts the burden of supervisory responsibility.

One supervisor's department had a high rate of turnover. It seemed he always was desperately looking for replacements. As a result he'd grab anyone, promise to give the employee what he wanted, or overstate the job. In no time he'd get someone to "work the problem." The trouble was that the transfers in soon transferred back out. Typical reasons were "I don't like the work," "I didn't get the promised raise," "The work was too hard (or too easy)," "That job wasn't what I expected." The department became nothing more than a revolving door. When the supervisor finally dismantled this merry-go-round, he learned to:

1. Interview for what he wanted.
2. Make promises that he could keep.
3. Accurately describe the job—the bad with the good.
4. Reduce his reliance on other supervisors' glowing recommendations.

Internal transfer is an excellent way to set the stage for promotions from within. Rotation programs are too. But be sure that the candidates are screened and meet company performance standards. If you do, the transfers you make will reflect positively on you.

LAYOFF

Layoffs can involve an individual or an entire group. Laying off an individual is often tougher. How do you handle it? One way is the blunt approach: "Joe, your last day is Friday. Good luck, fellow. Don't call us, we'll call you.'' That says it all—but it's pretty cruel. Contrast that kick in the pants with an organized program in which Joe, his co-workers, and you work together to help Joe find another, perhaps better job. It is possible to change a layoff from a devastating end to a challenging new start. Remember too that some apparent reasons for layoff (a temporary shortage of work, machine failure, personality conflicts) may be more appropriately solved by transfer.

Plan out how you will handle a layoff before you have to face it. When you anticipate an overstaffed position, act early. Identify the most likely layoff candidate so that the layoff will not come without warning or be harsh. Give your department the advantage of early warning too. You can do this in several ways:

1. Anticipate changing workloads. Reschedule or redistribute assignments so all idle time falls on one position.
2. Post notices of lost business opportunities that directly affect your department.
3. Announce changes in product mix.
4. Openly discuss the effect of new capital equipment on the department's workload.

Recognize that normal supervisory bias may be working on you. Unless you must follow a union seniority list, you will most likely lay off people you don't know (new hires) or don't like (marginally productive employees and people with personality problems). Don't decide too quickly. Be objective in your selection. Attempt to keep your most productive employees, whether you like them or not.

Be alert for opportunities to manage the layoff. Keep in mind that many companies provide income assistance allowances to employees who are laid off. Research, evaluate, and apply your company's policy. Establish payment schedules for the convenience of the laid-off employee. The dollar payout could go from full salary for some prescribed number of weeks to partial salary as a supplement to unemployment insurance payments. Most company-generated payments are tied to the number of years of continuous service—anywhere from one to 25 years or more. Although the payout formula is set by policy, there may be something you as supervisor can do to change it.

A supervisor can do more than follow the procedures manual. He can show his commitment to human relations by becoming personally involved in helping his subordinates find jobs. Once you decide to lay off an employee, you may find this nine-point program helpful. The objective of the program is to help you work with the employee at a time of stress, encouraging him to continue to believe in himself and his abilities. Here are the nine steps:

1. Handle the layoff notice properly. Present it as a manageable matter of fact, not as the end of the world. You can point out that it is not the employee's fault, emphasizing reasons unrelated to personal performance. Stress economic factors, reduced demand, seniority system, increased mechanization, or computer utilization.

2. Assess the employee's strengths and weaknesses. Help the person objectively identify his likes and dislikes, interests, and skills—and relate them to the local marketplace. By working with the employee, you can help him define a specific job he can seek.

3. Help the employee write his résumé. Résumé outlines are readily available at your public library. Match employee skills and preferences to a specific job definition. Make the résumé a rifle shot instead of a shotgun blast—be specific; not general. You don't have to be a creative writer. You do have to be factual.

4. Offer to rehearse the new job interview with the employee. Many laid-off employees haven't had an interview for some time. Practice sessions will sharpen them up and prepare them for those "hard" questions. For example: "Why did you leave your previous employer?" "Were you laid off?" "What can you offer me on this job?" "What are your greatest skills?"

Another useful approach is to have the employee interview for jobs he doesn't want. Although this may appear to be a waste of time, it really isn't. The benefits are reducing pressure, obtaining more experience in answering questions, handling that "nervous" feeling, and increasing poise and confidence. These benefits can be carried over into the "real" interviews.

5. Suggest that the employee learn all he can about a prospective employer before the job interview. As a minimum, he should learn about sales history, products, type of ownership, and union affiliations. This information may help the subordinate identify where he can specifically help that firm.

6. Consult rather than console. Make time available to the departing employee to discuss interview results. Routinely review progress on the job placement program. Stress results. If you are able to personally recommend the subordinate, help him find job openings through friends, clubs, and other contacts you may have.

7. Develop employee awareness. Insist on a goal orientation. Set goals for interviews, dates for reviews. Prepare the employee for a systematic approach to the task. Emphasize increased awareness of high-potential opportunities. Be sure to stress good manners and politeness. Remind the employee to be on time, to write thank-you letters after interviews, and to promptly acknowledge kindness. Often good manners and simple courtesy will clinch a job offer—if not this time, then next time for sure.

8. Broaden involvement. Get co-workers to pitch in to keep morale up. As supervisor, you are in a position to line people up to type and reproduce résumés. Such an action, which gives co-workers the chance to fill in and help out, can be a powerful motivator for the laid-off employee. It gives him the feeling that the folks at the office or on the line are helping. It can relieve the frustrated feeling of "Why aren't they the ones selected for layoff?" and substitute an "I can't let them down" feeling instead.

9. Work to maintain the candidate's self-esteem. This is a basis for high performance, for winning behavior. Help people see themselves as valuable, worthy, and capable. Attempt to arouse a sense of "nowness." Make decisions now, take actions now. Direct activities to a high tempo. Tempo reflects personal power, control, and accomplishment and promotes enthusiasm. It wins jobs.

This program really works. Helping subordinates relocate saves time and money and reduces emotional strain for the departing employee. Early job placement benefits the company through reduced income assistance payments and lower unemployment compensation. In addition, positive supervisory involvement reinforces the respect of the laid-off worker, the department, the firm, and the supervisor.

Bear in mind that since their first job, people have become used to taking direction from a supervisor. Capitalize on this habit pattern of boss and subordinate working together. Make finding another job like any other task. By stressing a positive approach, you can build the employee's confidence. It's needed. Give the effort focus. An interested supervisor's counsel and direction can improve the employee's chances of finding a new position. I'm not suggesting that you supplant the employee's judgment, just that you supplement it. Working together also builds empathy and objectivity. You're not abandoning anyone to fate or luck. You are working together for positive results.

TERMINATION

Never substitute layoff, an action that implies recall, for termination, an action that ends employment. If you have a situation that demands final action—take it. Termination takes two forms: voluntary and involuntary. Each raises the specter of severe supervisory problems.

Let's look at the "I quit" declaration first. Despite the problems associated with the resignation of an experienced subordinate, the separation presents the supervisor with several opportunities. These include:

- Finding out pay scales at the new firm.
- Recognizing a 50–50 chance of getting someone better.
- Utilizing a promote-from-within policy that recognizes other department members.
- Checking on how well the old employee followed company and departmental policies.

Of course, serious problems can also occur. For example:

- You may be tempted into a bidding contest. This has mixed success.
- Another subordinate may be lured away by the departee.
- Others in the group may get itchy feet and start looking elsewhere.
- In the termination interview, the departee may burn his bridges and make unsupported allegations about you.
- A replacement employee may cost more, throwing your salary structure into disrepair and forcing you to adjust other salaries.

It's good practice to plan ahead before someone quits. You should known in advance the answers to these questions: "What do I do if X quits?" "What action do I take if X goes with a competitor?" "Can I release X and waive the notice period?" "Is Y ready to take over?" "Should I be cross-training Z?" "Is there someone in another department who will help us over the transition period?" As you answer the questions, you will automatically develop an action plan.

You can help maintain department productivity by indicating your interest in the person leaving. Why? The two-week-notice period is a criticial one. Few departing employees will work as intensely as they did before the announcement. They have mentally quit and are eager to start their new job. Often a supportive supervisory attitude makes the difference between two weeks of highly productive work (including overtime) and two weeks of work that upsets and distracts others in your department.

Firing a subordinate is the final solution to a performance problem. Before you take this step, carefully examine your company's policy manual and consult with personnel experts. Current legislation on human rights and equal opportunity places a burden on the employer to prove the legitimacy of your action. At a minimum, you must build a solidly documented case of nonperformance of duties over a long period of time. The burden of proof is on you to show cause for dismissal. This is especially hard if the employee is over 40 and has been with you for some time. Of course, the performance reviews, events reporting, and other reports we will discuss later will help complete this file. But additional fact-to-face meetings and documented consultation sessions are also required.

Yes, you can still fire subordinates, but only after they've had a thoroughly fair chance to do their job. I recommend that you informally test your case in house beforehand. Otherwise, you may find yourself before a judge in court. Why? Because an employee's personal file may carry favorable references from previous supervisors. The case may boil down to an accusation that you apply unfair labor practices. A positive solution is to meet with the employee and genuinely work to solve problems. If termination is the only answer, try to allow the employee to resign. Sometimes offering an extra two weeks' pay is incentive enough to turn a "bridge burning" situation into a matter-of-fact parting of the way.

A sound employee separation program can help everyone. It takes the fear out of employee confrontations, generates improved morale, and improves productivity for the rest of your staff. As you learn how to handle separations fairly and objectively, your boss and your staff will recognize your concern for human relations. Separations are never easy, but they can be managed directly and confidently. The end result is a big plus for you.

PART II

Develop
Communication Skills

5

Make Ideas Worth Everybody's Time

As supervisor, you'll soon notice that you don't have time to do everything you'd like to. Your time is limited. You make yourself available to subordinates, yet they continuously make remarks like, "I know it will work. If we could only get his support." Other remarks often overheard at the water cooler are "He doesn't want to change anything around here," "He never has any time for me." Are people saying that about you? If they are, what can you do about it?

Don't automatically assume that you are doing the best job possible for yourself, your people, or your department. If you aren't creating an environment for new and better ways to do things, you are failing as a supervisor. Are your subordinates submitting their fair share of new ideas? Do you hear and support all the good ideas they generate? Is there a winning way subordinates can present their ideas to you? What can you do to improve the situation?

You can capitalize on the fact that time is limited by giving your employees an outline of how you prefer to receive their ideas. First, ask them to state the idea in one sentence. Second, have them put support concepts into line behind it. Third, have

Portions of this chapter are reprinted, with permission, from *The Toastmaster*, the official publication of Toastmasters International, Santa Ana, California. © 1975.

them organize available facts and research behind the support concepts.

Fourth, ask subordinates to stress their most important points. Newspapers put headlines at the top of every story to catch the reader's attention. So should your subordinates. Fifth, ask for redefined data. Get the benefit of your employees' analysis. An unorganized pile of words is very difficult to understand. Numbers are tougher. Point out that their chances of success are improved if they don't lead you through the same maze of data they went through to reach their conclusions.

Suggest that the first draft of the presentation be completed as quickly as possible—in one sitting if possible. Employees can then sit back and edit the draft. Tell them to decide if they've emphasized positive or negative thoughts. Have them rewrite, reorganize, and polish it. They should read their material aloud and dry-run it for friends or co-workers to see how it sounds.

All data should be brief and to the point. The alternatives are unthinkable. A dignitary visiting Brazil for the first time appeared before a large gathering of natives. He launched into a long, rambling story. It went on for the better part of a half hour. The audience listened respectfully. When he finished, his interpreter rose and said six words. The natives laughed uproariously. The dignitary was stunned. "How could you tell my story so quickly?" he asked. "Story too long," said the interpreter. "So I say, he make a funny. You laugh."

What you are trying to do is obtain usable ideas from your subordinates. To do this, you need tact and diplomacy. Take a lesson from the sergeant who went to Tact and Diplomacy School for a year. The day he returned to his base, his commanding officer approached him carrying a message. The conversation started, "Well, sergeant, how did school go?"

"Super," answered the sergeant. "I really learned how to use tact."

"Glad to hear that. We've just received notice that Smith's grandfather passed away. Go in and tell him."

The sergeant entered the barracks. He paused at the doorway

and shouted, "Attention." When all were in line, he ordered, "All those with living grandfathers step forward. You may stand still Smith."

GENERATING IDEAS

To get more and better ideas from subordinates, you must make it worth their time. Whether a subordinate likes or hates you personally, he will generate positive new ideas if you can show him how they will help him too. So organize your approach. Discuss it with subordinates. Take the time to listen to subordinates' suggestions.

Where do subordinates' ideas come from? They find them wherever they are. If they are alert, interested, and motivated, they will find new ideas in everyday experiences. They find ideas because they see things from their own particular viewpoint. It may be different from yours, but that shouldn't automatically color it bad. Because their perspective is different, they can find something where you see nothing.

To help your subordinates get ideas, have them ask "what if" questions. What if we do it this way? What if we do it that way? Have them relate the past to what they hear, to their future plans, and to their profession or field. Often their ideas may come as stimulating questions. Ask yourself, "Why should a subordinate think about improved methods?"

Let your subordinates know you want their ideas and suggestions. Tell them the kinds of ideas you are likely to accept. Indicate what else you need to know. Be sincere; convince them. Put yourself in their shoes. Would you believe it if you were your subordinate? To be believed, you must reward ideas. Even a pat on the back will do.

Ideas may hit your people when they see you make a mistake. Have you ever tried to get a boss to reverse a decision? Have you ever said, "Hey, boss, you're all wet on this one?" Can your employees tell you when you are wrong? What do you do about it? A "thank you" is best.

Sometimes it may be more valuable to have subordinates stress a key point they want to make rather than to think their ideas through fully. This approach puts a lot of the load on your shoulders. The advantage is that you can determine how far to take the idea to make it serviceable before any effort is wasted. On the other hand, you may prefer that employees provide all kinds of support data, rationales, and arguments. You must decide what you want.

When you present the idea to your boss, you must compete with his other concerns to get his attention. How do you get it? Are you anything like the lion that ate a bull? It felt so superior that it roared and roared. A nearby hunter heard the racket, came upon the lion, and killed it with a single shot. There is a moral: When you are full of bull, keep your mouth shut. If the noisy approach works, use it. In many cases it won't.

PRESENTATIONS

You should clearly specify the form of presentation that is best for you—oral or written, with or without visual aids. Are you better as a listener or reader? What alternatives do you want explored? Do you want to hear cost and profit implications? Should new insights and challenges to the status quo be considered? Your subordinates aren't mind readers, so tell them what you want, before they waste their time and yours.

A formal presentation may be required for implementing major changes. The presentation can be structured to attain a specific objective. You must help subordinates recognize management's real objective. An East Coast firm wanted to increase profits. The budget director was invited to listen in on the marketing manager's budget plans and to criticize them. The budget manager's implied objective was to reduce costs, which would increase profits. He was delighted when the first proposal called for a $100,000 budget cut. When the marketing manager described his second proposal, an even bigger budget cut seemed likely. However, the marketing manager surprised everyone when he pointed out that the plan added $200,000 to his budget. He gave a logical step-by-step analysis on the basis of expected market expansion. He demonstrated that the firm would actually increase profit by $500,000 by spending another $200,000. The premise: We want to make more profit. The president approved the second plan. The real objective was not to reduce expenses but to increase profit. This formal presentation with factual support convinced the decision maker that spending was the best way to reach it.

Are you a "cutter" or a "builder"? Ideas for change generally rest on facts. Facts work for you. Several years ago I was able to reduce the assessed valuation of my property by thousands of dollars. I presented my case to members of the city council. They changed my assessment on the basis of "facts they hadn't ever thought about." I had presented facts in a way that carried my "idea." I was able to prove that my residence was truly different from other residences. The logical presentation of data obtained from the city engineer and from texts in the local library changed a city policy.

What is your real goal? Is it to get usable new ideas or to keep things the same? A change orientation means you've got to do something. It means you want to identify problems and evaluate potential solutions. A status quo orientation tends to keep creative people frustrated. It doesn't move your department toward something better.

To get ideas in today's world of changing employment attitudes you must combine your talents—you must be engineer, manufacturer, and salesman. You must polish all your skills, publish your objectives, and identify with your subordinates.

As you work with subordinates to get ideas, stress the importance of enumerating alternatives. Explain why each must have support. Point out that supportive data must be accurate and complete. You may not need to use all the information but you need to have it organized and ready. It will enable you to answer your boss's questions and will increase your chances of selling the idea. Identify the sources of your information—give others full credit for their work. This will build the confidence of your staff. It also gains support for your idea from the people or departments that helped you.

IMPLEMENTING NEW IDEAS

You can't implement all the good ideas you will receive. Some require a decision from your boss or "higher-ups." Help your subordinates analyze your customer market. Tell them all you know about your boss's attitudes, habits, wants, likes, and dislikes. And keep researching. Be sure that the support data you request will answer the question he usually asks. A sure one is: "What's in it for me?" Bosses are people too; they need some benefit to offset the risk of sponsoring an idea. So think like your boss. If you know what he considers important—cost, profit, or ego—you can shape your presentation to cover it. This sounds like extra work. It is. The payoff is saving time and getting your idea accepted.

The timing of a presentation can be crucial. The best idea, with all the support in the world, will not be implemented if it is proposed at a bad time. You can check on the timeliness of your ideas by dropping a hint, testing the water, whetting an appetite. If you get a nibble, tell your people to get the complete package ready. Set a deadline for having all the information available. I've found that many ideas are most effectively presented orally, with support schedules supplied for later reference. Tell employees to make themselves available to handle questions. Having the creator of an idea available to answer a critical question can be a great time-saver and idea-saver too.

Submitting ideas carries risk. So if you want subordinates to give you ideas for change, the time to start laying the groundwork is now. Issue clear objectives. Identify benefits to the risk taker too.

Implemented ideas help other ideas grow. One success leads to two, then three. Point out that subordinates need to help you understand their ideas (maybe even save face). The presenter may know more about the subject than you. Ask for patience. Recognize that the real test of a good idea is when you begin to think it's yours.

You have to be a catalyst if you want to capitalize on the motivation and technical knowledge of your subordinates. In addition, you must develop an understanding of individual behavior and couple that understanding with effective, to-the-point training. If the ideas you sponsor are successful, everyone should benefit. You can then reap the rewards.

6

Bring Your Presentations to Life

As supervisor, you are expected to stand up in front of various groups (subordinates, peers, and management) and talk. How do you rate yourself as a speaker? Are you comfortable talking to a group—of friends, co-workers, superiors, strangers? As a supervisor you will have a chance to be heard. Will you make the most of your opportunity?

There are several kinds of speeches. They range from extemporaneous words on the weather to a well-planned, highly polished presentation to sell a new product, idea, or policy. Presentations can be the building blocks for your career—or they can become cement that holds you in place.

CREATING CONCRETE PICTURES

To be effective, presentations must create concrete pictures. Transparencies (slides) used with an overhead projector provide an inexpensive way to depict your ideas, and they can be changed quickly and easily. If used properly, transparencies offer several benefits:

Portions of this chapter are reprinted, with permission, from *The Toastmaster,* the official publication of Toastmasters International, Santa Ana, California. © 1977.

1. They provide a visual outline of your talk.
2. They help you control audience attention.
3. They can be used without dimming room lights.
4. If transparencies are mounted on frames, you can write notes on them, hidden from the viewer.
5. Color transparencies enliven a presentation.
6. Overlay transparencies highlight data relationships.
7. The graphic use of words and numbers enhances understanding.

Unfortunately, there are a few drawbacks too. To find them, put yourself in the seats with your audience. Can each clearly see your pictures? Does your text relate to the transparency? Do your pictures enhance and illustrate your message?

There are at least seven general types of transparency users. We'll discuss each. Which type are you?

Type 1 is the speaker who has color transparencies of outstanding quality. This supervisor obviously takes his speaking assignments seriously. He has invested a lot of time, care, and expense in his presentation. He obviously understands how to use color to highlight his major thoughts. He uses overlays too. But despite this outstanding effort, there is a significant problem: By slide 3 the audience can tell he is reading his notes. Word for word. He's out of touch with the audience. The highly polished slides alone are not enough to hold people's attention. This speaker spent all his time polishing and perfecting his slides. The result? He didn't know his speech.

Type 2 is the busy speaker who doesn't take enough time to prepare his presentation. His overhead slides are simply copies of the typewritten pages of his speech. The colored backgrounds are especially distracting to the audience. To make matters worse, the typewriter ribbon used was about shot and the print is almost illegible. This supervisor finishes himself off by presenting financial information. Data. Numbers. Numbers in columns. Numbers in rows. Percentages.

The audience gets two things from this supervisor. First, a

case of eyestrain; second, a headache. Why? Because anyone who has the patience to concentrate on reading the slide loses the speaker's words. The poor quality of the visual aids further detracts from the message. The speaker could have helped himself by testing the slides before he used them. He could have reviewed his slides on the screen in the conference room and evaluated his presentation. If he had, he would have eliminated most of the numbers, using only those vital to his major arguments.

The type 3 speaker uses neat, well-organized slides in easy-to-read boldface type. They appear very professional and businesslike. Each slide is limited to about ten lines of text. So far so good. If he stays with one slide and uses it as an outline, his presentation will go well. Instead, for one 12-minute speech he uses 12 transparencies. He uses notes too. Of course, his notes are a carbon copy of the slides. How do you know? Because he finishes his talk without ever looking at the audience, using his slides as a crutch. This fainthearted supervisor's message is wasted. The audience can read faster than the speaker can verbalize. His speech is a race. Guess who loses?

The type 4 speaker uses good-quality slides and has a flair for the dramatic. He produces a pointer as he starts his talk. With it he indicates the part of the transparency the audience should read. It isn't long until he has turned his back completely to the audience and begins to duel with the screen. The scene is exciting to watch. The highlight comes when he stabs a hole in the screen. It doesn't die, though—the speaker does.

Type 5 is the speaker who believes in the informal approach. He uses handwritten slides to put people at ease. A very cost-effective approach. Unfortunately, penmanship was not his best subject in school. His slides are half printed, half written. The writing on the wall says, "Don't do it!" Why? Because if you know your subject, *no* slides are better than poor ones. Poor slides impair the oral message. Its tough enough to hold an audience without having to compete with disturbing visual aids.

The type 6 speaker uses an effective mixture of slides—some with pictures, others only with words. This supervisor knows that word slides will highlight his major points. He uses summary word slides to open and close each topic. The picture slides are excellent illustrations of the fine points being discussed. Alternating different types of slides allows the speaker to arouse, and maintain, audience interest. A pattern develops which assists the audience. As arguments are presented, the speaker goes from (1) major theme to (2) presentation of proof and benefits with illustrations to (3) summary. In effect, the supervisor packages his long presentation into several short ones, giving the audience the full impact of each supporting point. Effective use of visual aids paints concrete pictures. They help the speaker and audience stay together throughout the speech.

Type 7 is the speaker who uses word slides only—no pictures. Each slide contains one main thought. This alone can set the stage for creating mental pictures. He understands that the primary reason for using visuals is to aid the audience. (The speaker is expected to know what he is talking about.) This supervisor keeps his main points readily available to his audience. He uses slides to introduce a subject and capture audience attention. Once a subject is introduced, he turns the machine off. Now the audience must concentrate solely on him. When he needs to help the listener recall the major point, he restarts the projector, points out how his remarks relate to the subject, and again turns off the machine (as he "turns on" to the audience).

The type 7 speaker avoids the traps of complicated, unrelated, illegible, and competitive aids. Since he is expert in his subject, he talks from his points to the audience. Every remark relates directly to his point. As a result, each statement builds upon the previous one and becomes the introduction for the next. The flow of his message is not interrupted. He maintains eye contact with members of the audience, forcing them to concentrate on and follow him. This supervisor knows how to establish and maintain coordination of speaker, topic, visual aid, and audience. He is a concrete example of how to avoid being cemented into place.

POLISHING YOUR PRESENTATION

These seven supervisors illustrate some right and wrong approaches to using visual aids. Which one are you? The next time you are called upon to give a well-planned, highly polished presentation, remember to:

Know your subject thoroughly.
Use concrete illustrations.
Speak—don't read.
Help your audience visualize to keep them interested.

Your next speaking opportunity may come sooner than you think. If you can use an overhead projector, do it. By combining your knowledge with simple visual aids, you can give your message impact. Statistical data suggest that words plus pictures aid audience recall. Concrete illustrations (mental and visual) will pave your career path to success.

7

Remember to Supervise Meetings Too

As supervisor you'll soon find yourself in great demand. You'll be invited to all kinds of meetings. Not to be outdone, you'll want to invite others to meet with you. But don't overdo it. Why not? Because meetings are expensive.

Do you know what meetings are costing your firm? Have you ever evaluated meeting results in relation to meeting costs? Was your last meeting really worth what it cost? If your answer is "Never thought about it," or "I don't know," you'd better start doing some serious thinking about the role that meetings play in your communication system.

Of course, meetings can be important to the operation of any department. It can be argued that a well-conducted meeting:

Delivers information to a group quickly and directly.
Reduces the chances of misunderstandings.
Saves time spent in writing and answering letters.
Gets an immediate reaction.
Uncovers new ideas.
Relaxes tensions and improves teamwork.
Produces timely decisions.
Provides a forum to resolve conflicts, disagreements, or questions.

Adapted, by permission of the publisher, from *Supervision,* a publication of the National Research Bureau, Inc. © May, June 1977.

Exposes participants to other management levels.
Pays for itself.

Make up your own list of benefits. Is increased profit one of them? Time invested in meetings should be profitable. Unfortunately, too many meetings are big losses. They waste the time of all attendees. High-salaried people find themselves sitting through two- and three-hour meetings merely to answer minor questions that could have been handled by a simple phone call.

ANALYZING MEETING COSTS

Most people will readily admit that much of the time they spend in meetings is not productive, but only a few have seriously attempted to define or eliminate the problem. These people are promptly labeled "unreasonable" or "overachievers." Actually they are cost-effective supervisors. Such a trait will help them advance in management stature.

You can analyze meeting costs quite easily. Table 7-1 depicts salary costs for a one-hour meeting of up to ten participants. Notice the entry of $100 an hour. What is the average per-hour cost of your meetings?

Table 7-2 identifies the number of dollars tied to labor costs

Table 7-1. Salary cost per hour for meetings.

		1	2	3	4	5	6	7	8	9	10
	10	10	20	30	40	50	60	70	80	90	100
	9	9	18	27	36	45	54	63	72	81	90
	8	8	16	24	32	40	48	56	64	72	80
	7	7	14	21	28	35	42	49	56	63	70
Average	6	6	12	18	24	30	36	42	48	54	60
Salary	5	5	10	15	20	25	30	35	40	45	50
($/hr.)	4	4	8	12	16	20	24	28	32	36	40
	3	3	6	9	12	15	18	21	24	27	30
	2	2	4	6	8	10	12	14	16	18	20
	1	1	2	3	4	5	6	7	8	9	10
	0										

Number of Participants

Table 7-2. Additional fringe cost per hour for meetings.

	100	5.00	10.00	15.00	20.00	25.00	30.00	35.00
	90	4.50	9.00	13.50	18.00	22.50	27.00	31.50
	80	4.00	8.00	12.00	16.00	20.00	24.00	28.00
	70	3.50	7.00	10.50	14.00	17.50	21.00	24.50
Total	60	3.00	6.00	9.00	12.00	15.00	18.00	21.00
Salary	50	2.50	5.00	7.50	10.00	12.50	15.00	17.50
Cost	40	2.00	4.00	6.00	8.00	10.00	12.00	14.00
($/hr.)	30	1.50	3.00	4.50	6.00	7.50	9.00	10.50
	20	1.00	2.00	3.00	4.00	5.00	6.00	7.00
	10	.50	1.00	1.50	2.00	2.50	3.00	3.50
	0							
		5	10	15	20	25	30	35

Average Fringe Percentage

at various fringe benefit rates. The fringe cost percentage provides for holiday, vacation, sick leave, group insurance, retirement plans, FICA, and unemployment insurance for the participants. At 25 percent (a low value), the $100 from Table 7-1 grows to a total cost of $125 per hour.

Table 7-3 adds an anticipated general administrative cost factor. This is added to help find the total costs to be recovered—similar to marking up production costs. At a 14 percent value, another $17.50 per hour is added to costs. The total cost involved in the sample one-hour meeting is $142.50 ($100.00 + $25.00 + $17.50). And still no factor has been added for profit! Table 7-4 summarizes the calculations from the three preceding tables.

A cost control program is essential in a well-managed department. In your cost control program, challenge the cost of meetings. As you do so, don't overlook hidden costs.

HIDDEN COSTS OF MEETINGS

It is important to accurately identify all of these—the costs associated with planning, site selection, agenda, invitations, coordination of schedules, and visuals (slides or transparencies).

Table 7-3. General administrative cost per hour for meetings.

Average Salary and Fringe Cost ($/hr.)	2	4	6	8	10	12	14	16	18	20
125.00	2.50	5.00	7.50	10.00	12.50	15.00	17.50	20.00	22.50	25.00
112.50	2.25	4.50	6.75	9.00	11.25	13.50	15.75	18.00	20.25	22.50
100.00	2.00	4.00	6.00	8.00	10.00	12.00	14.00	16.00	18.00	20.00
87.50	1.75	3.50	5.25	7.00	8.75	10.50	12.25	14.00	15.75	17.50
75.00	1.50	3.00	4.50	6.00	7.50	9.00	10.50	12.00	13.50	15.00
62.50	1.25	2.50	3.75	5.00	6.25	7.50	8.75	10.00	11.25	12.50
50.00	1.00	2.00	3.00	4.00	5.00	6.00	7.00	8.00	9.00	10.00
37.50	.75	1.50	2.25	3.00	3.75	4.50	5.25	6.00	6.75	7.50
25.00	.50	1.00	1.50	2.00	2.50	3.00	3.50	4.00	4.50	5.00
12.50	.25	.50	.75	1.00	1.25	1.50	1.75	2.00	2.25	2.50
0										

Average General Administrative Percentage

Table 7-4. Total cost to support a one-hour meeting.

Salary Cost (Table 7-1)	Fringe (Table 7-2)	General Administrative (Table 7-3)	Total
100.00	25.00	17.50	142.50
90.00	22.50	15.75	128.25
80.00	20.00	14.00	114.00
70.00	17.50	12.25	99.75
60.00	15.00	10.50	85.50
50.00	12.50	8.75	71.25
40.00	10.00	7.00	57.00
30.00	7.50	5.25	42.75
20.00	5.00	3.50	28.55
10.00	2.50	1.75	14.25

These costs and many more are involved in having a meeting and could easily more than double basic meeting costs.

What are some specific hidden costs of meetings? A brief review indicates the following possibilities:

1. Secretarial costs. These include reserving the room, ordering the coffee or rolls, and getting a projector and screen.
2. Waiting costs. I've seen 15 executives milling around for ten minutes because no one could produce a key to the conference room or because the "decision maker" was late.
3. Transportation costs. These include walking, driving, parking, taking trains, and flying.
4. Meal costs. If the meeting is held during breakfast, lunch, or supper, meal costs must be added.

And don't forget what's happening at your desk while you're attending a meeting:

1. Your paperwork is gathering dust. Who does your work while you are gone?
2. Your telephone slips are piling up. When you do return

the calls, you may find that your caller is in a meeting. Result: You leave a call slip for him. And over and over.

3. You calendar stays crowded, forcing you to rush from one place to another.
4. Your co-workers are planning an evening with their families. Too bad you can't. You have paperwork to look forward to.
5. Who is coaching your subordinates while you are gone? Are they being cheated by your absence?
6. If yours is a service group, can you be sure you are effectively providing the required service by attending meetings?

Putting a price tag on missed opportunities, hurried decisions, and employee discontent and error may be impractical. However, they do produce costs.

Even in cost-sensitive recessionary periods, at any moment tens of thousands of people are tied up in meetings—meetings that should be measured for profitability but aren't. In fact, one wag defined a recession as a time when sales are down 5 percent, but meetings are up 25 percent.

FORM A MEETINGS TASK FORCE

Many companies periodically form task teams to reduce expenses for telephone, travel, paper, reports, and so forth. Budget reductions and manpower realignments are commonplace. Then why not a meetings reduction task force?

Could it be that the irony of having to *call* meetings to reduce meetings prevents management from starting this effort? It shouldn't. As I've suggested, the potential savings are well worth the effort. As a cost-conscious supervisor, can you afford to overlook any idea that can increase productivity?

Get started today. Form a task force. Budget $5, $10, or $20,000 for it. Target savings at ten times budget. The task force can:

Figure 7-1. Meeting log.

			Scheduled Start Time _____
Place: _____	Subject: _____		Actual Start Time _____
	Meeting called by: _____		End Time _____
			Elapsed Time _____

Date	People Present	Department Represented	Achievements/Action Items	Assigned To	Due Date

Figure 7-2. Meeting questionnaire.

Subject of Meeting

Name of Originator

IF YOU ORIGINATED THIS MEETING, ANSWER THE QUESTIONS BELOW

A. Are other meetings required to complete this subject?

Yes _____   No _____

Other Sources for Data	Could Be Received From
1. _____	_____
2. _____	_____
3. _____	_____

B. Estimated preparation time for this meeting

Your time_____(man-hours)

Others' time _____ (man-hours)

C. Should this meeting be eliminated or reduced in size, cost, or frequency?

Yes _____   No _____

Explain _____

_____

This Space for Task Force Use Only

Reviewed by_____   Date _____

RETURN TO:_____ (MAIL STATION) _____

Purpose of Meeting
_____

Length of Meeting
_____

IF YOU ATTENDED THIS MEETING,
ANSWER THE QUESTIONS BELOW
_____

A. Will this meeting be used to call other meetings?

      Yes _____   No _____

  Identify Additional Meetings:

              Scheduled Meetings Dates

	Date	Time	Agenda Due:
1.	_____	_____	_____
2.	_____	_____	_____
3.	_____	_____	_____

B. Did you need to be at this meeting?

      Yes _____   No _____

C. Should meeting participation be reduced?

      Yes _____   No _____

  Explain _____

  _____

D. Should meeting format be changed?

      Yes _____   No _____

  Explain _____

  _____

E. Length of time you think meeting should have taken:

  _____

F. Meeting was used to:

  Give Information _____ Get Information _____

  Other (Identify) _____

G. Suggestions to Improve Meeting _____

BY: _____ (DATE) _____

Devise meeting control forms.
Identify problems and hidden costs.
Issue directives.
Mobilize employee involvement.
Get results.

Figures 7-1 and 7-2 are sample control forms. The "meeting log" is used for a predetermined test period (perhaps 30 days). Each meeting leader is required to complete it and send a copy to a meeting coordinator, named by the task force. His job is to summarize the data for presentation to the task force.

The "meeting questionnaire" is completed by all attendees and submitted to departmental coordinators. They in turn prepare summaries for the time period and send them to the meeting coordinator, who provides the overall results to the task force. The objective is to get feedback on the effectiveness, productivity, and results of the meetings held during the test period.

Some problems seem to demand repetitive meetings. If a subject requires continuous discussion, Figure 7-3 may be helpful. Its purpose is to highlight problem areas so the task force can focus on alternative solutions.

The task force should be careful to avoid an overreaction. This could suppress the vital exchange of interdepartmental information. The emphasis must be clearly on communicating effectively, not on cutting down communication.

OTHER MEETING PROBLEMS

Many supervisors and managers have developed poor meeting manners. The task force can help improve their conduct by creating a code of meeting manners. For example, the task force can direct individuals to:

1. Accept meeting invitations only if they have bona fide reasons for being there.

Figure 7-3. Repetitive meetings control summary.

Submitted By	Location	Department Name	For Period From To		
				Estimated Savings	
Meeting Subject	Originating Department/Date	Prep. Time (man-hrs)	Recommended Reduction		
			Change Frequency	Eliminate	Reduce Prep. Time (man-hrs)
			Dollars	Effective Date	

2. Insist that the leader be prepared and have definite goals for the meeting. Require detailed agendas.
3. Establish priorities for actions discussed.
4. Get each action item assigned to one person and agree on review and completion dates.
5. Decline the invitation if insufficient notice is given and suggest a more appropriate time.
6. Be sure that someone is responsible for taking notes and for getting the notes distributed the next day.
7. Give the meeting a time limit; then keep the group moving. Respect participants' car pool or bus schedules.
8. Always leave instructions with someone in the office so they can be contacted if necessary (Some may want to leave instructions to be called out in 30 minutes.)
9. Notify subordinates of their participation in a meeting.
10. Evaluate the group leader, participation, and results. Did the leader establish goals? Is another meeting required? Should different people be involved? Is the discussion complete? Is anyone responsible for action? Does he or she know it?
11. Be polite and concise.
12. Avoid using profanity.

Participants should also be alerted to the tactics often pulled by meeting "bad guys." These people:

1. Invite others without regard for their duties and priorities.
2. Have their secretary leave the invitation on the invitee's desk so that the meeting becomes an unwelcome surprise.
3. Call the meeting for nonbusiness hours or weekends.
4. Never issue an agenda.
5. Fail to announce the subject of the meeting.
6. Fail to say who will be there.
7. Fail to bring any records with them and hence are unable to answer anything.

8. Drop a lot of "big names" of people who aren't there, implying that these people support them.
9. Use technical terms that no one understands.
10. Sit in the back of the room or away from the table to show they don't agree with the group.
11. Avoid facts; act on rumors and impressions.
12. Keep the group droning on and on without letting anyone leave.
13. Always blame someone else for problems and never put themselves on report. (This is especially effective in front of customers.)
14. Argue and frown a lot to show they are serious. After all, they want to be known as problem solvers, not as humorists.
15. Use negative statements in talking about others. (But they are positive when referring to themselves.)
16. Bring up irrelevant material and trivia, then deliver it in a somber vein.
17. Challenge you to prove anything you say.
18. Delegate their participation by sending someone in who has no authority to act or speak for them.
19. Use obsolete data to support their position.
20. Run out on meetings they called, leaving everyone wondering what to do next. The answer is to leave.

Granted, at times one or more of these tactics may be required because of the extreme urgency of the situation. However, if they become common, the meetings probably will not produce profitable results.

GETTING RESULTS

One sure way to get results is to shorten or cancel waste-of-time meetings. Here are some suggested guidelines:

Limit discussions to business matters. Do not replay yesterday's ballgame. Remind yourself that every minute wasted is multiplied by the number of meeting attendees. Don't recap for the latecomer. People should not be penalized for someone else's bad manners. Let the latecomer catch up.

If the person calling the meeting is not prepared, ask him to reschedule and adjourn the meeting. Keep discussions oriented to meeting objectives. Don't allow the meeting to get sidetracked on extraneous issues. There is a natural reluctance to embarrass the meeting leader, especially if he's the boss. So a request for unsigned written comments or questions may get more complete and open participation. This also eliminates having to listen to an endless succession of questions that are irrelevant to many of the attendees.

Keep invitees to a minimum. Be like the kindergarten student who told his mother, "There will be a very little PTA meeting tomorrow night. It's just you, me, and the teacher." Also, don't allow for any breaks. Schedule the meeting right through lunch. Even the most persistent talker can be brief when faced with growling stomachs.

Bring a tape recorder and announce you are taping everyone's comments. If someone becomes abusive, ask him to apologize. If he won't, ask him to leave the meeting. If he doesn't, you leave. Another good tactic is to close all conference rooms for specified times during the day.

The most effective personal meeting shortener is to say no. If you can contribute nothing to a meeting, say so—and don't attend. Otherwise, you may be scheduled as an audience your entire day. In addition, you can set a personal limit on the amount of time you spend in meetings—say, 1, 2, or 4 hours per day. And before you call a meeting ask, "Do I really need all this participation?"

As part of an overall meeting cost reduction program, find substitutes for meetings. Develop policies on when to have one and when not to have one. Meetings follow a 90–10 rule: 90 percent of the time is spent on relatively unimportant matters, 10 percent on key items. A well-written report can take the place of many meetings and do it at a lower total cost.

The bigger the company, the greater the need for meetings.

Therefore, big savings from cost reduction programs are more likely in larger firms. One research study found that the most effective meeting size is five participants. When the group gets larger, the leader's efforts to get results are hampered. Small meetings are more likely to get prompt results than large ones.

If the group gets above 13, the meeting has become a conference. Conferences tend to discuss rather than decide. You should develop rules of thumb on the size of the group you want and the type of meeting to hold.

Analyze the meetings you have recently attended. Do the same people seem to call most of them? Why? Are they insecure, overly dependent, inept? Do you always see the same people? Have they inadvertantly formed a "club" that makes little progress? How many people from each department attended? If more than one per department, why? Did just one or two people do all the talking? Was the meeting used as a training or burial ground? (You know the kind—one mistake and you're dead!)

As you concentrate on the guidelines listed above and make them part of your routine, you will help everyone become more conscious of meeting costs. Spending less time in meetings will give you more time to plan and organize your work.

Set a target. If you could cut the time spent in meetings by 10 percent, how much could you save your firm? As we saw earlier, eliminating a one-hour meeting each day could save over $100. Cutting one hour out of one meeting each working day will result in a savings of over $20,000 per year! Get started today. Establish a task force. Slash meeting costs now.

8

Staff Meetings Can Be Fun

If you've never had a staff meeting, you're missing a great opportunity. Staff meetings are an excellent forum and provide a source of instant feedback.

A staff meeting can be a unique management tool, a vital communication link to your subordinates. It can be one of the most significant business meetings you hold. The meeting can be a quiet gathering when a harried supervisor meets with crew for a friendly chat. Or it can be an emergency session to solve a crisis. Whatever it is, before you call the meeting, prepare for it. In this setting you can plan, organize, provide data, swap experiences—do anything that will benefit your entire staff.

If you already have staff meetings, analyze them. What was the specific purpose of your last meeting? Did it accomplish its objective? Was your staff involved in the discussion, or did you do all the talking? Did you relate to the group and they to you? Was any productive work accomplished? Was the meeting as valuable a communication tool as you expected?

If you answered no to many of these questions, you may have a problem—one shared by many supervisors. You may have failed to realize that special controls are needed to keep staff meetings on the track. Unless a meeting is controlled, it can turn into a waste of everybody's time. Bear in mind that a "Dagwood sandwich" satisfies no one. In this kind of meeting everyone has his mouth open but no one bites into the subject. To have productive staff meetings you must do three things:

Set meeting controls.
Productively use any objections raised.
Stress group and individual benefits.

CONTROLLING STAFF MEETINGS

In order to control meetings, you must establish the right meeting climate. By this I don't mean room temperature. Aim for a congenial, constructive give-and-take atmosphere. If successful, it can improve the interpersonal relationships of your team members. Then decide on frequency. Should you have meetings every day, week, or month, or is once a year enough? Bear in mind that the meeting must be perceived as a productive use of time. There are two rules of thumb you can follow:

1. If your department's environment is changing rapidly, meetings should be frequent.
2. If most items are routine or data are available from other sources, meetings can be held less frequently.

You must also decide the kind of meeting to hold at any given time. Some meetings will be informational—for getting and giving facts. Others will focus on making decisions, exploring alternatives, or gathering facts. Some may merely be social events for storytelling.

Special-purpose staff meetings can be called at any time for any reason. The special session should have a significant reason for being. Generally it is a one-subject meeting. It may involve a reorganization, a customer problem, or recognition of the efforts of an individual. If necessary, have each staff member come prepared to work the specific problem. Announce the subject in advance to give people time to uncover facts, gather data, and prepare possible alternatives. (You improve your chances of getting factual, up-to-date data if you give adequate warning.)

Another special reason to have a staff meeting is to obtain specialized data. At the same time, you can develop speaking skills of staff members, who will be asked to present material about a subject of interest to the entire group. This can be an effective way to measure the ideas, abilities, and talent of each staffer.

Routine informational meetings keep your staff up to date on procedures, new employees, policy revisions, and other items. Use such routine meetings to cover "state of the department" topics and to keep people informed. You do most of the talking. These meetings can be formal or informal. It's your choice. If formal, they can include such items as reviewing minutes of old business, introducing new business, action plans, and people responsible. Distribute an agenda before the meeting so everyone can be prepared for discussions.

Staff meetings are a valuable tool for developing the supervisor's ability to listen. Supervisors talk, cajole, complain, direct, inform, create—but rarely listen. Inattention speaks louder than words. It shouts, "I don't care what you think. My mind is made up. Don't bother me with facts." Thus listening for feedback is a valid objective. Does your staff know if it individually or collectively has your approval? A staff meeting gives you a real chance to indicate your support of the group and to maximize rapport with your staff. If you miss this chance to bring the group closer together, you create a climate where objections can flourish.

OVERCOMING OBJECTIONS

Without proper control, staff meetings can be disasters. Here are some of the most common objections associated with them:

1. "Meetings are too long." If the subjects don't require as much time as you allow, your meetings will be described as a waste of time.

2. "Staff meetings are dull, boring, and monotonous. They have no significance." If your meeting is merely a rehash of last week, trivia will soon take precedence over tomorrow's actions.

3. "The meeting is nothing more than crying and laments. All we talk about is how tough things are." This gripe is evidence of low morale. Faced with a constant diet of "we can't" topics, your most positive staffer will quickly become demoralized.

4. "In our meetings the boss harangues us over and over again about his pet topic. Who cares? He's already covered his feelings with each of us. Who needs it again?" If a problem isn't resolved to your satisfaction, drop it for a while. It will be easier to resolve in a fresh approach later on.

5. "It's Monday morning. So we go to staff, whether there's anything to discuss or not." This fixed routine gives your staff the impression that you meet because it's Monday, not because action is required.

6. "I don't know what he's talking about." You can create considerable confusion in a staff meeting if your language is vague. Every participant may leave with a different interpretation of what was said. Be specific. Keep instructions simple.

7. "He's against everything we propose." If you constantly override your staffers, they may conclude that you are against them. Result: They won't support you either. If you must go against your staff, discuss your reasons.

8. "He introduces a subject then tries to start a fight." Unless you are careful, you can create jealous splinter groups or destroy closely knit teams. A wrong word or an ill-timed glance can demotivate staffers.

9. "Time is wasted rehashing past successes without relating them to new problems or opportunities." If you live in the past, your organization will not be ready to face the future.

10. "Time limits are not set. No priorities are established." As a result, no one can tell what is urgent.

11. "The boss uses his staff as an audience to demonstrate how great he is. He delights in ridiculing one or more staffers."

Result: Staffers will do anything to avoid being noticed and will try to outdo each other in risk avoidance. No one wants to be the butt of a supervisor's mean humor.

12. "He's holding out on us. He isn't telling us the whole story. I've been set up again." In some staff meetings the staff does not get any information. The result is hurt feelings and irritation.

13. "These meetings are nothing more than Joe and Moe showing off. I sure get tired of hearing those guys get undeserved praise." Note: Whenever one or two staffers talk on and rarely say anything helpful to the group, you've lost control of the meeting.

14. "Staff meetings always degenerate into a fight." Is your staff meeting a place for informal discussion of ideas, or is it a series of duels to the death?

15. "He never decides anything. He uses the staff meeting to try to get a consensus." This dilutes management responsibility and weakens the leadership role.

16. "The staff meeting is used to get facts and facts and more facts." Do you spend all your time fact-finding, or do you spend time deciding?

You can probably identify many more objections. To hold successful meetings, you must work to overcome every objection. This requires careful planning, control, and management of the meeting.

STRESSING THE BENEFITS

Properly conducted staff meetings can benefit everyone involved. Which of the following benefits are your subordinates receiving today? Your staff meeting can be a chance for them to:

1. Give presentations, gain valuable speaking experience, and obtain your approval.

2. Learn about and/or set a "party line" on a subject, policy, or procedure.
3. Obtain information on management topics.
4. Debate pros and cons of key issues in a "friendly" atmosphere.
5. Observe the proper way to conduct meetings.
6. Learn new policies.
7. Plant ideas with peers.
8. Compete for new or different assignments.
9. Become involved in the decision-making process.
10. Simultaneously share the experiences of several supervisors.
11. See how conflicts are resolved.
12. Obtain a sense of group unity.
13. Receive special attention for exceptional achievement.
14. Discuss variances from group targets.
15. Become equals in a meaningful work relationship.
16. Report on the status of assignments that affect the entire group.

A staff meeting can be a strong link in your communications chain. To be sure yours are positively shaping your group, you should hold mental postmortems. Ask yourself what went well and what didn't. Benefit from your experience. Remember, too, to pick your spots. Have staff meetings only as often as they are beneficial. In some months you may need to call brief daily get-togethers. In other months, only one meeting will be plenty.

Make your staff meetings an integral part of achieving your objectives. Staff meetings must stimulate the activities of your subordinates. Create an environment that involves your staff. If you can, toss in some information and how-to-do-it instructions, and require performance reports. To avoid wasting time, you can limit discussion on each report.

Locate your "hidden agenda"—those unstated reasons you do what you do. Tie them into your published program. Smoke out as many other hidden agendas as you can. Most people will not give you the real reasons for their actions or beliefs. But if you listen closely you should be able to identify them. Then take steps toward building a solid team attitude.

By setting goals, minimizing objections, and maximizing benefits, you will create a positive setting for your staff meetings. Bear in mind that your results are the summation of your staff's. Start today to increase the value of your staff meetings. As you do, you will make these meetings more pleasant for everyone.

9

Reports Should Work For You, Not Against You

Hardly a day goes by without some foreman, supervisor, or manager issuing a report to "management." You probably issue quite a few too. Are your reports influencing decisions, or are they being used as scratch paper by the boss's Sunday School class?

Some reports are dull, routine. These are repetitive statements in a set format sent to a standard distribution list, covering a specific time period, generally aimed at one subject, and distributed on a standard schedule because they contain data that someone may require.

You should have a goal for each routine report. The goal should be to generate an action or to update the status of a current product, project, program, or problem. The report should be action-oriented, a statement that pinpoints problems. To clarify your position, expand on the data and shape them around recommended solutions.

Routine reports don't cover everything. Some events are so important that they can't wait for the next scheduled release date. Thus "exception" reports are required too. I call these

Portions of this chapter are reprinted, with permission, from *CGA* magazine, March 1978, published by the Canadian Certified General Accountants' Association. © 1978.

"situation summaries." (See Figure 9-1.) They are like routine reports except that they require:

1. A problem statement or action proposal.
2. A recommended solution or action, including the benefits (to whom, when, how, why, what, and where).
3. Support data, rationale, and analysis.

A situation summary *forces* action. Thus it is more than a routine status report. It focuses management action into a narrow range of acceptable responses. The format shown in Figure 9-1 can be effectively used in verbal or oral presentations. It will organize your thoughts crisply to cover all elements critical to the management decision-making process.

MAKE YOUR REPORTS LOOK GOOD

There are many kinds of reporting activities. They can be categorized as follows:

Routine or situational.
Required or volunteered.
Cosmetic (how do I look?) or scare (this is awful).
Verbal or oral.
Formal or informal.
Fixed format or variable format.

A 100 percent scrap report is a routine, required, scare, verbal, formal, fixed-format report. A rumor that the plant manager has decided to start a third shift is a situational, volunteered, cosmetic, oral, informal, variable-format report.

Several factors will influence the type of reporting you select. These include you (your strengths and weaknesses), the requester, time requirements and schedules, data scope, degree of accuracy required, and urgency. When you respond to a request

Figure 9-1.

Situation Summary
(or Record of Telephone Call)

Date:_____

Time: _____

Subject: _____

Program/Project/Product:_____

Problem: _____

_____

_____

Recommended Solution: (include pros and cons as attachments)_____

_____

_____

Alternative Solutions: (include pros and cons as attachments) _____

_____

_____

Related Requirements: Products, Processes, Plants _____

_____

_____

Customer: _____

People Involved: _____

_____

Financial Summary

  Benefits _____

  Costs_____   _____
                                        Issuer
                          Telephone Extension_____

for information, you decide which type of reporting is most appropriate.

As you prepare reports for the normal communications channel, keep in mind that today's managers possess varied backgrounds, skills, interests, and training. Some have no experience in your field and have no interest in learning about it. This means that raw, unprocessed data that you think make an obvious point may not get any reaction. The detail work is your job. Managers expect you to tell them the facts in time to take corrective action.

Reports don't always stay where you send them. They do get sent "upstairs." Under the right circumstances a report can shoot up like a rocket. This is particularly true when an unsolved problem is highlighted. Be ready. Make sure your reports look good. Covers can be descriptive and useful. A good cover tells more than words and pictures. It hints that the contents will be well organized and easy to understand. Good marketing people understand the importance of product packaging. Be sure your reports are effectively packaged.

A real challenge to supervisors comes in determining what information will really help management. Why? Because routine reports define activities that regularly get management attention. A manager can only manage what he sees—or what he thinks he sees. If proper information is not available—or available but mistimed or misrepresented—management will have to make its decision without adequate data. Don't become the scapegoat for a bad decision.

Somewhere in your developmental process you must learn to present data clearly, creatively, objectively, and positively. Managers don't like "bad news," but they will tolerate it (and the messenger) if it is presented carefully. Reports can lead to deeper examinations of the organization, task force studies, or changes in strategy, product mix, and production lines. Don't be the messenger who loses out because he is unable to artfully present data that call for a change.

As a supervisor, you issue reports every day. Your status reports compare something (spending rate, efficiency, productivity, number of new hires) against a plan or against the same period last year. They can also measure performance on an existing development project. Are they doing their job? To make sure they're on target, listen to what others are saying. For example, one of your senior executives may ask, "What should I concentrate on now? My financial people tell me I should be worried about turnover ratios, revenue per employee, return on assets, and productivity factors. Where do I find them? Will they help me to do the best possible job of managing my part of the business? Who is responsible? What do I control and manage to make them better?"

Get the message? Carefully examine your reports. Try to orient them to answering these questions. That's right. Listen for questions. Don't be defensive. Make your reports answer questions *before* they get asked. Systematically develop and implement routine reports that answer the questions management normally raises.

One way to learn management's most likely questions is to interview several tiers of managers. Perhaps you can get invited to status reviews given by others. Listen to the questions and find the answers that are *accepted*. If one answer leads to another question, answer it too. If a question is obvious to you, do yourself a favor and answer it before it is asked. Also recognize that new managers may have different needs from their predecessors. And they haven't been around long enough to become confident in your work. Be ready to change your routine. Change should be part of your routine.

The sweatshop, production line, Simon Legree supervisor of yesterday is nearly extinct. Today's supervisors are measured on more than productive output; they are expected to be forward-looking, astute, goal-oriented people. To succeed in this role, you must be an active observer who produces effective reports. You can do so by:

Establishing a goal for each report.

Specifying how the report achieves the objectives of management.

Choosing the "best" medium.

These steps will lead to better internal reporting, which promotes more effective management. With any luck you'll get as a by-product better communications, up and down.

RULES FOR EFFECTIVE REPORTING

There are a number of general rules to follow in producing any report—whether it is hurriedly jotted on the backs of envelopes or printed in color on the highest-grade glossy paper. To begin with, be sure to use language that the current management team understands. Each department in the company has its own buzzwords and slang. Forget the way things were done at your last employer. And speak in simple, straightforward, easy-to-understand terms. Be alert for confusion. The engineer and the accountant may attach a different technical meaning to the same word.

When key data are presented in a standard format, using company terminology, managers don't have to constantly develop new bases of understanding. They begin to feel confident in and comfortable with the data. This eases the decision process—and helps your chances of moving into the inner circle too.

Use a single data source, and be sure all data can be traced to that source. Pick a source that can be audited or verified. This goes for "material-move" tickets, sales journals, cost ledgers, design releases, budgets, sales orders, or shipping documents. Also, keep the costs of reporting down by using the same data in more than one report. In doing so, you underscore how some information is involved in more than one business decision or covers more than one level of management. The result is improved communication.

Enhance the data by giving management the benefit of your

analysis. Without adequate interpretation, a pile of data is useless. Do not issue unrefined data unless you are specifically
requested to do so or unless time limits prevent analysis. Identify what is important, even if you can only circle a number or
write in a question mark. Develop a report that concentrates on
measuring and evaluating outputs. Analyze inputs when outputs
substantially differ from what was planned or expected.

Get the report out fast. If you are preparing a long report,
don't wait for all the information you need. Issue an early,
abridged edition or use estimates for critical information. Follow up later with the complete edition when information for all
schedules has been processed.

Expand upon your analysis as needed. Any unusual data call
for editorial comment. A footnote can be used to give depth to
your news. As a rule of thumb, footnote the cause of at least 70
percent of any variance. If a problem has been solved, use footnotes to describe its current status. Describe corrective actions
undertaken and events still being completed. If a problem isn't
solved, generate a solution. Recommend alternative approaches
and assign them priorities. It's good management practice. You
can also use footnotes to discuss side issues and to answer objections and questions. A report that raises more questions than
it answers only creates headaches.

Make comparable data really comparable. When "apples"
are compared with "oranges," the "fruit salad" argument that
follows confuses everyone and wastes time. This lesson was
driven home to me early in my career: Under our budget, the
first fiscal month had 20 workdays, but no holidays. In fact, the
company had three paid holidays in April. Employees filled out
their timecards correctly. Thus when the actual labor charged
out was compared with budget, three days appeared to be missing. It seemed to be an obvious computer error. As a payroll accountant, I spent many hours trying to convince irate managers
that the payroll was correct. No one questioned the budget. It
had been reviewed and approved by everyone in management.
We were all quite embarrassed when a junior payroll clerk dis-

covered that the "approved by management" budget was the problem. The actual data reported was correct, but not comparable to the budget.

Similarly, base differences, usually caused by reorganizations, can make comparisons with earlier plans useless. Instead, restate the prior period. It's the current organization you're interested in measuring. Use footnotes to explain adjustments, especially if assumptions about the past are necessary.

Comparisons of current year with prior years can mislead management too, especially if the accounting periods contain a different number of workdays or fiscal weeks. Look out for four- versus five-week months, variable holidays, 52 versus 53 weeks. Be consistent. Decide (or get direction) on how to depict current year and other years, actual and planned results. Stick with the same format on all reports. Make column-to-column comparisons easy by using the same headings and order. Avoid this:

1980			1979		
Variance	Reported	Plan	Plan	Actual	Variance
200	1000	800	900	950	50

Always explain any numbers in parentheses. Tell if variance is "better" or "worse," "bad" or "good." Use tables of contents when appropriate to help people quickly locate segments of information. (See Figure 9-2.) A contents page is especially useful in long reports with a lot of supporting schedules. It is a good organizer for you and a sure time-saver for the recipient.

Credit your information sources in your report. As part of the reference, indicate the date of the data and the names of people supplying opinions or conclusions. You can quote individuals, but use good manners. Discuss statements with people being quoted first. Send them a copy of the report. You may have misunderstood or misquoted.

Be sure to put your name (initials) and the date prepared on

Figure 9-2. Sample table of contents for a report.

all your report pages. This simple step avoids many needless arguments later—for example, when someone else produces a different answer based on a different source. By identifying yourself and your sources, you build user confidence in your reports. You actively show that you are trying to work with others in an open, information-sharing environment.

Always insist on quality control. Do you check your work? Does someone else? Usually it's easier and more effective to have another person check your work. He will find obvious, easily-overlooked adding and typing mistakes—*those that you gloss over because you are familiar with the data.* In addition, the checker can make sure that all the rules we've discussed so far have been followed. If he questions your interpretation of support data, do not take it as a threat. Your objective is to produce accurate reports, consistent in format and technique, and to put your best work forward.

Make your reports easy to read and file. Select a vertical or horizontal format, and stick with it throughout the report. You'll find a friend in every manager who reads and secretary who files your reports if you three-hole-punch them before distribution. After punching the holes, make sure that no data were accidentally cut out. A report with missing numbers will irritate users.

Challenge routine reports regularly. Reports that have stopped doing their job should be discontinued. How do you know your management needs the information? One way is to stop issuing it. Who misses it? Why? Follow up personally if junior-grade administrative people complain. Many administrative staffers happily keep each other busy sending unnecessary data back and forth.

Careful supervisory review is needed to ensure that only meaningful data are reported. Interview recipients, audit source details, and evaluate other reports. Chances are good that you'll find some report that duplicates all or part of the information yours contains. Challenge both reports. Make each justify its existence. After a reorganization (management change), find out if the new management wants or needs the old report. This step can save considerable time, money, and frustration.

Why spend all this effort to ensure that reports are current, meaningful, accurate, timely, and useful? To get the right data to the right people at the right time. Think of the report as your product—designed, developed, and packaged to customer specifications.

DYNAMIC REPORTING

To achieve its goals, management must be given information when it can be used profitably. Thus reporting can be categorized according to three time divisions: "before," "as," and "after."

"Before" reporting anticipates the future. It includes forecasting results, summarizing Delphic probes, making breakeven analyses, identifying trends, preparing PERT charts, estimating product costs, and playing the "what if" game. Quantitative analysis and close teamwork have an important role in the design, development, and production of this type of report. The result could be a five-year plan, a new product business plan, or a set of strategy statements.

"As" reporting monitors daily variances from cost standards, labor efficiency, cash flow, material usage, parts shortages, delinquent accounts receivable, sales, and shipments. Much like a thermostat turning a furnace on and off, this type of report causes an action to happen.

"After" reporting covers historical operating statistics. It includes income statements, balance sheets, ratio analyses—the whole body of data called financial reporting. It also covers overhead rates, labor standards, patent applications, time-and-motion studies, and the development of baselines for establishing future operating goals.

Reports should be dynamic. They should anticipate tomorrow's decisions, monitor today's, and measure yesterday's. When they do, they create an "under control" management environment for your company. Demonstrate your concern for dynamic reporting by keeping on top of changing needs. Interview new managers as they are appointed. Get their contrasting views, requirements, and recommendations. Talk to project engineers, foremen, people in their first supervisory post. Discuss reports that are available. Explain how they should be used, what they try to accomplish. Repeat the process. Watch for trends. Don't allow your reports to become obsolete. Management may decide that you are obsolete too. At best, you'll be considered unimaginative.

If you supervise a financial function, make sure you explain how generally known financial performance measures apply specifically to your firm, division, or cost center, or to a single supervisor. Make sure that management understands the financial components of its decisions. Help management associate overall summary performance with identifiable areas of responsibility. The emphasis changes in engineering, sales, and production, but the principle remains the same. Be sure you understand how to meaningfully relate your expertise to management.

Make sure your reports reach their intended audience. If most of your documents are stuffed into an envelope and "tossed in over the transom," you're probably having little impact. Look at alternatives: personal delivery, special meetings, exception distributions. Make it known that you are available to explain and answer questions. The personal touch can improve your visibility and enhance the impact of the report.

One final thought. Just as a salesman has a catalog of his products readily available, so you should maintain a catalog of your routine reports. Such a catalog is handy when you are training new employees, briefing new managers, or deciding which reports to challenge. A sample catalog might contain:

Table of contents
Sample pages
Reason for the report
Key items

Report synopsis
Release date
List of recipients
Sources of data
Preparing department

The reporting system described in this chapter will help bring your achievements closer to your goals. It will place you in the forefront of measuring and monitoring management activities. Your commitment to reporting understandable results will increase your impact in the company. Your reports will work for you to influence decisions. One of the decisions could be to promote you.

PART III
Evaluation Techniques

10

Give Credit Where Credit Is Due

One of the most rewarding tasks facing the large organization today is devising a system of management that consistently yields timely and constructive results. This objective becomes increasingly difficult as the number of people and functions in the organization increases.

One of the resulting problems is that almost no one seems to ask or do anything because he wants it. Every request for action or for information is directed at *someone else,* generally someone higher in the organization.

To find ways of overcoming the apparent absence of commitment and the inability to get desired results, keen observers have monitored, analyzed, documented, and interpreted actions of people working in industry. Such well-known researchers as Peter Drucker, George Odiorne, and Dale McConkey have come up with "management by objectives," "management by results," and the "integrated management system," all attempting to improve the productivity of the worker.

These principles have been applied with success by a group of financial analysts working in the Division of Financial Analysis and Control (DFAC) in the treasurer's function of a computer manufacturing company. They developed a system with the basic goal of giving people credit where credit is due. Their purpose was to overcome many of the problems people have in relating to their work. The general structure of the comprehensive credit system is shown in Table 10-1.

Determining how to give and take credit for results is a tough problem for a company, its supervisors, and individual participants. Making the system work in an environment of rapid change increases the challenge. As a case example, let's look more closely at DFAC and its work environment.

DFAC AND ITS WORK ENVIRONMENT

DFAC has three subsections—financial analysis, overhead control, and divisional reporting—each headed by a department supervisor. (See Figure 10-1.) DFAC's primary function is to provide the financial information and analysis needed to responsibly and profitably manage the division. It is, in effect, an extension of the chief financial executive's office. A top management point of view is applied to routine operations as well as to special projects.

DFAC personnel work with a wide range of special interests, plant locations, and levels of authority in the process of prepar-

Table 10-1. Structure of DFAC credit system.

Measurement Criteria	Routine Tasks	Special Objectives	Long-Term Objectives
Original documentation	Personal calendar of events	IMS Objective	IMS Objectives worksheet
Schedule monitoring	Reports control board	IMS Objective, follow-up copy	IMS Objectives control board
Results reporting	Weekly reports status summary and monthly calendar-of-events summary	Weekly significant-events report	Quarterly evaluations

Figure 10-1. DFAC reporting relationships.

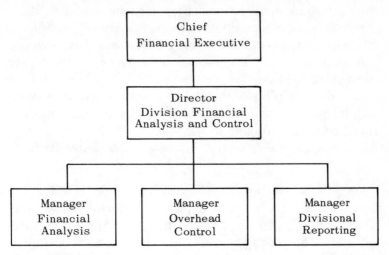

ing management reports, financial plans, forecasts, and other materials. If we view the division as an orchestra, DFAC's task is to be the arranger, to assemble and blend the distinctive tones of each instrument to produce a harmonious progression of sounds and to functionally support the conductor.

DFAC's close working relationships with the treasurer and general manager often lead to requests for comprehensive and accurate projects, completed on short notice. In anticipation of these requests, analysts in DFAC must keep up to date on activities both within the division and outside—in areas that may present opportunities or threats for the division. They must also maintain good rapport with people who can provide reliable information from their fields of interest. DFAC sometimes enjoys the luxury of having a reasonable time to do a thorough study, but it is more likely to be asked to respond immediately or sooner. Using the orchestra analogy again, it must be ready for improvisational "jam sessions" as well as well-rehearsed concerts. In either instance, of course, the final "score" will be reviewed by a number of critics.

DFAC also has routine work assignments—tasks such as controlling interdivisional cost transfers, preparing accounting statements for home office consolidation, and developing departmental budget reports. In these areas, the emphasis is on accuracy and consistency—and documentation for the ever present, ever questioning auditors.

In a division of more than 6,000 people, DFAC provides a vital interpretive communication link for departmental and divisional concerns. Working in this dynamic environment can be devastating or rewarding, depending on how people respond.

REPETITIVE REPORTS AND ROUTINE ITEMS

In earlier experiences with a management-by-objectives program at DFAC, routine tasks were often ignored or given secondary status. People assigned to these tasks found it difficult to receive adequate credit for consistent, reliable performance. They were taken for granted. The new credit system tries to give the routine tasks clear-cut visibility. How? By maintaining a prominently displayed control board (3 feet high by 6 feet wide) for regularly issued reports and a calendar of events for all routine tasks.

The reports control board is a schedule that identifies due dates on all reports to be issued by DFAC for a two-month period. (See Figure 10-2.) Report titles and the names of individuals responsible for issuing the reports appear on $1'' \times 2''$ cards, displayed on the board under the required due dates. The cards are color-coded to indicate department responsibility.

Every Monday, each department reports on the status of reports due or issued the previous week. (See Figure 10-3). This information is posted to the control board, and one of the following is noted for each report:

> O = issued; on time
> L + (number of days late) = issued; late
> E + (number of days early) = issued; early
> N = not issued; requirements canceled

Figure 10-2. DFAC reports control board.

Financial Operating Results
H. F. Jones

FEBRUARY

1	2	3		6	7	8	9	10		13	14	15	16	17		20	21	22	23	24		27	28
E1	E2	0		0	0	0	0	0		0	0	L1	0	0		E1	0						
0		0		E1	0	0		0			0	0		0		0							
0				0		0						0											
						0																	

MARCH

1	2	3		6	7	8	9	10		13	14	15	16	17		20	21	22	23	24		27	28	29	30	31

Figure 10-2. DFAC reports control board.

Figure 10-3. Weekly reports status summary.

Division Financial Control Reports Issued, Week Ending FEB. 3

Report Title	Person Responsible	Date Issued	Early	On Time	Late	Remarks
Financial Operating Results	H. F. Jones	1/31		O		
Weekly Overhead Variance	R. P. Dales	2/1	E1			
Inventory Analysis	R. D. Carl	2/2			L3	Computer malfunction delayed source data
Capital Assets Additions	D. C. Mill			O		

The following reports, due this week, will not be issued:

The schedule board thus presents a constant reminder of what should be done next. It gives wide visibility to the report schedules, the people responsible for issuing the reports, and their effectiveness in meeting schedules.

(Note: Status notations are made with a china marker on a plastic covering over each card. These are then wiped clean for reuse in subsequent months.)

Expanding this concept to include all routine tasks and to provide a permanent record at the same time, DFAC added a personal calendar of events. As regularly scheduled and incidental tasks are completed, the person responsible makes a notation on a memo calendar. (See Figure 10-4.) At the end of each month, the individual calendars are collected and events and activities are matched to scheduled due dates. The comparison is submitted to department management for review, summarization, and analysis.

The monthly calendar-of-events summary, shown in Figure 10-5, includes statistics on such items as the number of events achieved early, the number achieved on time, and the number completed late. To round out the summary, detailed explanations are attached for events not completed on time.

These two procedures, one with weekly reporting and the other with monthly analysis, combine to make individual performance on routing tasks completely visible to management. Yes, the procedure takes some time, but the benefit is worth it. No one is taken for granted!

COMPLETED WORK OBJECTIVES

The DFAC director's goals and targets provide a framework for developing objectives for each of the departmental supervisors. Building on this base, the supervisors assess their level of contribution. As part of a divisionwide program called the Integrated Management System (IMS), they then develop plans for improving their effectiveness. Performance reviews are held

Figure 10-4. Personal calendar of events.

MONTH ___February___   EMPLOYEE ___H. F. Jones___

Monday	Tuesday	Wednesday	Thursday	Friday
		1 Issued Dec. Profit Forecast (E-1)	2 Made adjustments to Dec. Allocations (E-1)	3
6 Analyzed Dec. General Costs (O)	7	8	9	10
13	14	15 Received Dec. Financial Allocations on/DKC (L-1)	16	17 Completed Financial Operating Results (O)
20	21	22	23	24
27	28			

Figure 10-5. Monthly calendar of events summary.

	No. of Events	% of Total	Total Days Early (Late)
Division Financial Analysis and Control Calendar of Events—February 1978 Summary of Achievements			
Events completed early	33	29%	125
Events completed on schedule	58	51	0
Events not completed (See attachment for details)	13	11	0
Events completed late (See attachment for details)	10	9	(28)
Totals	114	100%	97

quarterly. New objectives are routinely developed for subsequent periods. Descriptions of objectives and performance in attaining them are kept on file. The written record provides support for salary reviews. (See Figure 10-6.)

To help bridge the gap between quarterly reviews and day-to-day operations, as new work assignments are issued, DFAC documents them. The written record may be initiated by either the employee or his supervisor. By mutual agreement it is entered into the formal system. The person responsible for the task receives the original of a two-part form entitled IMS Objective (see Figure 10-7), and his supervisor retains the copy for follow-up. When the task is completed, the original form and a summary report or statement are submitted to the supervisor. Comments on the quality and promptness of the results are added by the supervisor, and the forms are kept on file. They may be used for reference in weekly reporting of significant events, IMS Objective reviews, and salary actions. This simple, automatic process for keeping track of subobjectives, interim objectives, and special tasks is the key to DFAC's success at making IMS relevant to its work environment.

Figure 10-6. IMS Objective worksheet.

Name	Period Begins	Period Ends	Interim Performance Review Dates					
			Performance Appraisal					Performance Review Comments
			Exceeded	Achieved	Partially Met	Little Done	No Activity	
Accountabilities List in order of importance the end results your job must consistently produce.	**Job Objectives** Write objectives you expect to accomplish in the next realistic time period within the appropriate accountabilities. Objectives criteria: Very specific (quantify if possible); Timed; Attainable; Cover the entire job; Represent personal growth.							Note reasons for performance — at either extreme

Figure 10-7. IMS Objective form for nonroutine assignments.

IMS OBJECTIVE

Date _____

Name _____ Objective No._____

Report to _____ Due Date_____

Initial estimate of time to be spent on this objective _____ hrs.

Objective:

Date completed _____ Time spent on this objective _____

Evaluation of results:

In addition, DFAC displays each manager's most important objectives (thus establishing priorities) on a schedule board similar to the reports control board. This is another aid in monitoring individual accomplishments. Posted on this board are report due dates for a three-month period. Objectives or critical subobjectives are also listed, with corresponding target dates. A notation is made on the display board as each target is attained.

In addition to all this writing, the system involves considerable discussion. Objectives are discussed during interim monthly reviews and every three months. Formal, face-to-face evaluations are made at the quarterly IMS reviews. Each department supervisor meets with the DFAC director and objectively appraises his performance in relation to the objectives agreed upon at the previous review. Objectives are rated as exceeded, achieved, partially met, little done, no activity, or failed. Objectives that have not been achieved on time are examined to determine the reason for failure. Discussion is pointed toward the best way to get them completed. New target dates are agreed upon, and, if necessary, the objectives are redefined.

Again, as with the routine items, DFAC emphasizes visibility of results. The aim of the program is to promote prompt completion of work assignments and to provide a comprehensive baseline for allocating rewards.

SIGNIFICANT-EVENTS REPORTING AND SALARY REVIEWS

As part of its policy of recognizing achievements and at the same time keeping all levels of authority informed on departmental activities, DFAC has a weekly significant-events reporting procedure. It begins at the lowest clerk level and pyramids into a report issued by the treasurer to the general manager.

The events reporting begins on Friday mornings in DFAC. Each employee reports to his supervisor on the significant (nonroutine) events that occurred in his area of responsibility. The supervisors summarize and expand on items submitted to them. They issue their report, as does the director, and so on up the line. For the first-level employee, the reporting requirement may be fulfilled by submitting the IMS Objectives completed that week. (If a person fails to report, that failure is noted by the supervisor as a significant event.)

These reports, in addition to providing a timely flow of information to higher management, serve as an important historical record of departmental activities.

To vitalize the program further, DFAC links it to the concept of differential rewards. DFAC management feels that employee enthusiasm for meeting due dates and achieving job objectives would diminish quickly if performance were not related to rewards. While public acknowledgment and praise are not overlooked, financial rewards are especially important.

Salary reviews, of course, consider many factors, qualitative and quantitative. The documentation created in the DFAC credit system, when augmented by personal observation, provides a complete information base about an employee's work. It includes objectives, their difficulty, and how effectively and promptly each has been met. The process of giving credit where it is due through financial rewards becomes more precise and more objective with this broad base of data.

SUMMARY

The introduction of a system of results reporting often meets resistance from those who feel their jobs are too complex and dynamic to fit into a prescribed routine. Some will balk at any objective comparison of personal work assignments with others in the department. Also, some may be tempted to sacrifice thoroughness and high-quality workmanship just to meet due dates. For these reasons, it is important to make sure that primary emphasis, both in employee work habits and in management recognition, remains on the *quality* and *timeliness* of results. DFAC's system does not represent a cureall or a reordering of priorities; rather, it provides a systematic way of viewing and documenting the key elements of total job performance.

These additions to a standard Integrated Management System redefine its capability. They enable the system to effectively address the short-term objectives that develop between review periods and provide a way to monitor performance on routine tasks. By adding such things as weekly results reporting and display boards to the basic IMS procedures, DFAC has put IMS into the mainstream of management communications. These communications do have a cost, but it is not as high as you may think. The maintenance workload, which is mainly clerical, is estimated at less than an hour per week per employee.

DFAC believes that many of the conditions it deals with are the same as those faced in most administrative organizations. The approach can add new life to a management-by-objectives program in these environments. Why? Because it assures people that they get credit for what *they do!*

11

Subordinates Are Individuals Too

Yes. Subordinates are individuals too. And as individuals, they expect to be treated with respect and reason. This is especially true when they are being evaluated for salary adjustments. Whether you are a first-, second-, or third-shift supervisor, you can save your company a lot of money and yourself a lot of trouble by learning to emphasize your key role in evaluating individual subordinates.

Many supervisors tend to overlook their employees until a personnel problem surfaces. This allows misunderstandings to fester until they become big enough to affect boss-subordinate working relationships. Alert supervisors can prevent misunderstandings. Be on the lookout for opportunities to improve the climate for employee-employee and employee-supervisor communication in your company.

DO'S AND DON'TS OF PERFORMANCE APPRAISAL

An effective performance appraisal system is the basic building block of improved communications. Performance reviews are important and ought to be conducted frequently. They can be formal or informal. The informal review is essentially "coach-

Adapted, by permission of the publisher, from *Supervision,* a publication of the National Research Bureau, Inc. © January 1975.

ing"—a brief session that focuses on employee strengths or weaknesses as they occur in daily activities. Every task assigned, whether completed successfully or aborted, is an opportunity to coach a subordinate.

In addition to day-to-day coaching, many companies require formal quarterly, semiannual, or annual merit/performance reviews. Often appraisal summaries are tied to an employment anniversary or some other arbitrary date. Supervisory judgments are written up and filed in employee personnel records, and are used to justify salary adjustments. These documents represent the formalization of a supervisor's evaluation of his employees.

People conducting formal performance reviews often resemble Christopher Columbus. They get to the right place by accident. Columbus thought that he knew where he was going when he started. But when he got there he didn't know where he was, and when he got back he didn't know where he had been. Bear in mind that formal employee evaluations can be used to measure both the employee and the supervisor. Unless you carefully plan and map out your evaluation, your performance reviews may be just as disorganized as Columbus's voyage.

Here are some suggestions to improve the objectivity, quality, and acceptability of your reviews:

Do some coaching each day. Don't save up all the problems or all the good news for one big clout on "review day." Tell it the way you see it every day. Subordinates generally appreciate honesty and, like you, they don't appreciate surprises.

Keep a daily written record of each employee's specific achievements and contributions. Make it a habit to share your comments with subordinates. Focus on measuring the employee's development since the last review. Start each review period with a clean slate. People do change, often for the better.

Set aside plenty of time for writing the policy-required formal review. Schedule an uninterrupted period of time for presenting it to the employee. A rule of thumb is to invest the equivalent of one full working day for each employee review. Prepare the write-up in several sittings. Outline key points, using your notes. Describe accomplishments and employee personality traits and identify specific areas for improvement. Give examples. These can be as simple as recounting prior coaching sessions. Seem like a lot of work? It's not too much when you consider that you expect the subordinate to work about 220 days a year for you.

Remember that some employees don't want to develop and grow in their job. Decide whether that is acceptable. If an employee continues to be productive, don't make him miserable by insisting that he "grow" into a job he doesn't want. Finally, always try to be fair and objective. This won't always be easy, because you'll naturally like some people better than others. It's a matter of personality and chemistry. But as a supervisor you must learn to differentiate performance from the performer.

There are some absolute *don'ts* if you want to earn the respect of your subordinates:

1. Don't ask an employee to write his own review. The employee wants your appraisal. He wants to know how he measures up to your standards.

2. Don't avoid performance reviews. They provide a routine, scheduled way to establish open communication about work evaluation.

3. Don't write a review and then not discuss it with the employee. This practice breeds suspicion.

4. Don't be taken in by the "halo effect"—letting a few outstanding efforts near the review date influence your appraisal for the whole period. This is another reason you should keep records throughout the review period.

5. Don't rely on vague and general statements such as "He offers timely and worthwhile suggestions on critical problems." Get specific! What problems? Did they get solved? What suggestions? Were they implemented?

6. Don't play favorites. If your staff believes "politicking" counts more than performance—and pays better—performance will soon suffer.

SAMPLE PERFORMANCE EVALUATIONS

Let's look at a few examples of supervisory evaluations to see what effect they have on the employee. How would you feel if your work output and on-the-job performance were summarized like this?

> Since joining our organization in August 197X, Mr. A has been responsible for supervising materials planning and control. His major responsibilities have been supervision of three to four people handling coordination of materials pricing for proposals, government audits of materials proposals, purchase order audits, control of major equipment materials costs via system baselines, and monitoring of materials budgets. He has displayed a good attitude toward his job and has demonstrated supervisory abilities and willingness to accept new responsibilities.
>
> Most recently, in April 197X, Mr. A was reassigned to procurement. He is now senior buyer of integrated circuits—cores and diodes. Because of his short tenure, it is impossible to fully evaluate him under his new job responsibilities. However, he has shown the capabilities expected of a buyer, continuing to have a good attitude and an ability to pick up new responsibilities quickly.

That's all one manager wrote about a top-notch supervisor. His evaluation is little more than a set of general statements about general duties. If you were that subordinate, how positively could you react? Would the evaluation help motivate you to accomplish bigger and better tasks? Take on tougher challenges? Give you a feeling that your efforts are appreciated?

Another supervisor evaluated his secretary as follows:

> Mrs. B is very cooperative and cheerful in doing my work and also that of the technical planning department. The quality of her work is satisfactory.

The evaluation of a year's work in only 26 words! Do you think this will help Mrs. B do better than satisfactory work in the future?

A third supervisor wrote this about a senior cost estimator:

Mr. T, in only one year at LMN Company, had made tremendous progress. He is currently qualified to handle large, complex proposals and has demonstrated this ability on the current XYZ and ABC programs. He is extremely conscientious and has won the respect and admiration of his counterparts in contracts and systems. He willingly accepts all assignments and handles them efficiently and expeditiously.

In addition, Mr. T is extremely thorough and doesn't panic, despite tight schedules and adverse conditions.

Glowing terms for sure. But what did Mr. T really do? Where can he improve? Most personnel files (if they exist at all) are filled with vague, general records of employee performance. Perhaps that's why many firms don't even bother to maintain records of individual performance.

Contrast this apparent aversion to writing up specific performances with a review that goes into depth—one that attempts to thoroughly and objectively evaluate an employee's performance and to help formulate a plan for improvements:

Mr. A is a dedicated, hardworking member of the controller team. He was the program financial control analyst for the Buggy Whip market segment until April 1, 197X. On that date, responsibility within program financial control was changed and Mr. A is now responsible for the Horseless Carriage market segment. The programs under his supervision include 4- and 8-cylinder vehicles. These have a combined FY7X revenue value of $19 million. During the period being evaluated Mr. A was very active.

ACCOMPLISHED PERFORMANCE:
Mr. A's accomplishments include:

o Maintained an ongoing extensive analysis of Horseless Carriage product line of 4-cylinder vehicles, which resulted in accurate and timely statement of costs for the 21,800 units built to date.

o Designed and developed an estimate at completion in conjunction with factory operations and program management for the company-funded building program. This saved us $12,000.

o Designed and developed an analysis of inventory investment and situation summary for management authorization of 8-cylinder material.

○ Prepared a situation summary to recommend an estimate at completion and outcosting position on all basic contracts. The recommendation was accepted.

○ Identified $46,000 in mischarged product support costs. On his own initiative, transferred them to the product support account.

○ Resolved transfer of $139,000 in reconfiguration costs for the Straight 8 product line, with zero profit impact on us.

○ Designed and developed an analysis of V-8s that compares actual cost with sales price. This analysis will assist Department Z in supporting price comparisons with our competitors.

○ Prepared an analysis of the impact of treating facility costs as overhead costs instead of direct charges.

○ Issued 98 percent of routine reports on schedule.

TRAITS:

○ Mr. A is dependable. Completes required reports on or ahead of due dates.

○ He is independent. Takes independent initiative on special projects assigned to him. These include a special study of daily direct and indirect labor costs, and detailed analysis of Buggy Whip residual inventory.

○ Mr. A is thorough. Provides detailed and accurate analyses, including a V-8 estimate at completion and a Straight 8 facility cost analysis.

○ He is confident. Utilized new analytical techniques for a Polyfit program on V-8.

○ He is imaginative. Assisted the business systems group in enhancing and developing System M and System U.

DEVELOPMENT POTENTIAL:

Mr. A continues to improve his expertise. We have established a goal for him to develop a working knowledge of accounting concepts unrelated to program financial control. This will send him back to school two nights a week.

As a subordinate would you prefer to be evaluated as Mr. T or as Mr. A?

A secretary plays a vital role in your department. Can you afford to alienate her? The same Mrs. B mentioned before has changed departments. The next review in her file says:

> Mrs. B is the only secretary for the four professional employees in this department. Her primary responsibilities are to support one contract manager, two senior contract representatives, and one associate contract representative. Her specific duties include:
>
> o Typing approximately 1,000 outgoing contract letters and 100 TWX per year.
> o Processing about 800 incoming pieces of correspondence per year.
> o Making appropriate distribution of all applicable contractual information, letters, RFPA/A, PIF, and related material.
> o Making travel reservations.
> o Maintaining and applying knowledge of current company and department policies and procedures.
>
> Mrs. B is very proficient and professional in discharging her duties. She is willing to work additional hours to meet deadlines. Her dedication and initiative make her a valuable asset to the organization. We're pleased to count on her as a member of our team.

Would you guess that Mrs. B was more satisfied with the first or second review?

Would our cost estimator be better able to analyze his progress and evaluate where he stands in the organization by seeing this review?

> SCOPE AND ACCOMPLISHMENTS:
> Mr. T is the cost estimator for programs in the Air Force market segment. He is responsible for 60 Air Force programs that will generate $10 million in revenue this fiscal year. At his previous review, his responsibility covered 50 programs with $8 million in revenue.
>
> He has supported the functional organizations in preparing pricing system input. Through his expertise in systems planning, Mr. T has been able to assist the functional area with report explanations, verification of accuracy of input data, and general problem-solving ex-

pertise. He has helped management forecast contract funding requirements, which include forecasting spending plans and determining when additional customer funding is required to continue contract work effort.

During the review period, Mr. T utilized his systems background to take the lead role in preparing a cost growth proposal on the XYZ contract. His activities include:

○ Converting actual incurred cost data into a format that allows input into the pricing system.
○ Integrating PROMIS system planning into the pricing system.
○ Providing special analysis required by the proposal team leader.
○ Presenting our position to the customer during proposal fact-finding.

AREAS TO IMPROVE

Mr. T should take independent initiative to achieve a better understanding of the interrelationship between program cost estimating and the profit objectives of the division. He should attend the in-house workshop on budgeting for cost control.

Mr. T should work on developing an awareness of how his reactions to others may affect his effectiveness in working with them. We will assign him to task force Alpha. He should put more emphasis on becoming familiar with the capabilities available in new analytical tools, including the Maps system, Rims file, and Polyfit program. Joe J of the systems design group will be glad to help. The goal is to save Mr. T time in performing cost analyses.

Mr. T should make an effort to analyze the validity of incurred costs for programs under his responsibility. The analysis should include timecard checks, review of the functional organization's labor-charging procedures, and audit of expense reports and materials transfers.

Which type of review would you prefer to have in your personnel file?

The reader gets the feeling, in looking at the first examples, that these supervisors are uninterested or afraid to get involved. They use reviews like form letters, applying the same general statements, with minor modifications, to all their subordinates. The last examples are much more specific. They present a complete picture of each employee's capabilities. They try to identify the value of the individual to the company.

BE CONSTRUCTIVE.

Performance reviews should not rely completely on the supervisor's unsupported opinions and judgments. After all, these could be biased. Because face-to-face performance reviews are very personal, it is hard to establish one pattern for everyone. Each employee has different sensitivities, capabilities, and career objectives. Nevertheless, some generalizations can be made:

1. Try to avoid the "personality conflict." This is generally due to a failure in your approach. Be relaxed and open. Don't be defensive.

2. Stress job performance, not personal traits.

3. In discussing errors in judgment, find out what alternatives the employee considered before you make any judgment yourself.

4. Make your critique a learning experience for the subordinate. Illustrate from your own experience. You've made mistakes too; identify one or two and discuss how you solved them.

5. Watch to see how your comments are being received. If the employee reacts emotionally, you may want to let him "talk it out," stop for a cup of coffee, or reschedule discussion for another time.

Remember that criticism can be misunderstood. Be sure you are really being constructive. Organize your presentation around positive statements. For example, if given the choice between saying "Your poor performance is becoming a problem for me" and "Several aspects of your performance have impressed me," use the latter. It gives you an opening to cover both good points and bad.

If you expect your employees to perform well for you, you

must perform well for them. Make sure each one clearly understands your assessment of his performance, what you expect from him in the future, and what he can expect in return. Nothing destroys your credibility quicker than broken promises—whether real or imagined.

Performance evaluation is hard work, but it's well worth the effort. It can be the most useful communication tool available to you. By systematically following a logical program, you can improve your performance. More important, you can create a positive work environment in your department and a more productive work group. And that helps you too.

12

Try to Pay Them What They're Worth

Who is the most valuable member of your department? Who is the highest paid? Is it the same person? What about the No. 2, 3, or 4 performer? The further down the list you go, the more likely you are to find a glaring disparity between your judgment of a person's value to the organization and his or her salary ranking.

Any of several factors may be involved in creating rating inconsistencies. These include differences in length of service, changes in hiring practices, changes in performance measures, differences in growth potential, variations in company policy, and previous supervisory likes and dislikes. The important question is not "How did the disparity happen?" but "What can be done to change it?"

In rewarding employee performance, the instrument available for many supervisors is a formal salary review program. Increases or decreases in salary are based on periodic evaluations of individual on-the-job performance. But does that salary review program focus on individual progress exclusively? Or does it show some regard for the relative value of the individual to

Adapted, by permission of the publisher, from *Compensation Review,* Second Quarter 1974. © 1974 AMACOM, a division of American Management Associations. All rights reserved.

the department? This leads to a critical question: Can you afford to pay each employee what he or she is individually worth?

By routinely evaluating each employee strictly on the basis of personal development during the review period, you can easily perpetuate inequities in the organization's salary structure. You can create financial headaches as well.

What if you don't have a salary review program? How do you reward employee performance? There are several ways. Let's look at one of them. I led a team of financial analysts that tried to establish meaningful criteria to measure and forecast the dollar impact of salaries and salary changes on our firm. We used these questions and added several personal observations to lead us to a broader approach.

To recognize and realistically reward differences in performance, we argued that a firm should establish a budget for each employee. Then it could monitor each employee's progress—both in performance (productivity) and in salary. Comparisons could be made relating one person to other members of the work group—and to the firm's resources. Such a procedure would add continuity to the salary review process. It would also provide subjective and objective support for the difficult task of determining the proper salary for each employee within the limits set by prevailing economic conditions and management controls.

To accomplish our goals, we developed a practical monitoring process that made these factors visible to the supervisor of each department—or group of departments if functions were similar. The system is illustrated below, using data from a hypothetical organization with three departments (A, B, and C) reporting to one group manager.

PERFORMANCE RANKING

Each supervisor starts the process by ranking his subordinates according to his judgment about their value to his organization. A summary of these value ratings is shown in Table 12-1. This ranking may be done in other ways. You can select the measure

Table 12-1. Departmental ratings.

Department A			Department B			Department C		
Employee	Value Rating		Employee	Value Rating		Employee	Value Rating	
ACF	1		LOC	1		FMK	1	
DWM	2		DWY	2		WJN	2	
PDQ	3		MVA	3		JFT	3	
DDC	4		FJK	4		DWZ	4	
FRW	5		LEK	5		RLV	5	
KJL	6		IMC	6		RFG	6	
BMC	7		AGW	7		GRR	7	
			LBC	8		EGM	8	

that fits your situation. For instance, if you classify by salary grade, compare within grade; if you classify by job, use job.

Defining "value to the organization" can be difficult. It can vary from organization to organization because of differences in the type of work being done and/or differences in supervisory priorities. One approach is to decide which employee you would hire first if you were to start from scratch, then which one you would hire second, and so on. Or, if you had to lose an employee, you could decide who would go first, then second, and so on. Whichever method you select, make sure the appraisal criteria you use are reasonably consistent within your department. Consistency from year to year is also essential to make comparative value ratings meaningful. To the extent possible, they should be specific and objective rather than general and subjective.

What criteria can you use in developing your individual ratings? Appraisal can be divided into three areas: present job performance, growth orientation, and personal qualities. Some criteria for each of these areas are shown below:

PRESENT JOB PERFORMANCE
   Quality and quantity of work output
   Complexity of assignments
   Adaptability to new assignments
   Knowledge of company and industry

Application of past experience
Rapport with other departments and human relations
Achievements
GROWTH ORIENTATION
  Academic progress
  Application of unique talents
  Job-related uses of available time
  Initiative
  Communications training
  Desire for advancement
  Pursuit of professional credentials
PERSONAL QUALITIES
  Self-confidence
  Loyalty
  Persistence
  Patience
  Dedication to organizational goals
  Work habits and attitudes
  In-house political standing
  Dependability

Once the departmental ratings are completed, they can be merged into a composite ranking through a joint evaluation by the group manager and his supervisors. When a close working relationship exists between departments (that is, when each supervisor knows the personnel in the other departments well enough to personally evaluate them), the evaluation session can be kicked off by having each supervisor rank the entire organization. Obviously this step becomes more difficult as the number and size of the departments grow. In the composite group rating (Table 12-2), employees retain their departmental rating identification. For example, A-1 denotes the highest-rated person in Department A. Notice, too, that the supervisors doing the rating are excluded from the list.

A Delphi-type approach is used in developing the composite ranking. After the supervisors complete their first ranking of the total group, they are given a summary of the rankings for review. Each supervisor reevaluates his ratings in relation to those of the others. The supervisors discuss the rankings together and question one another. The goal is to reach agreement on the evaluations of individual employees. However, this process also stimulates interdepartmental work projects, and even job rotations.

As may be expected, in the early stages each department supervisor tends to rank his best performers at the top of the total group. As familiarity with the system and the personnel in other groups develops, however, more dispersed ratings occur.

An unexpected side benefit of this objective group rating is

Table 12-2. Group ratings.

Value Rating (1)	Employee (2)	Present Weekly Salary (3)	Salary Rank (4)	Absolute Variance (1)–(4) (5)
1	A-1	$ 400	1	0
2	C-1	325	4	2
3	C-2	360	2	1
4	B-1	295	8	4
5	B-2	340	3	2
6	C-3	300	7	1
7	C-4	280	9	2
8	B-3	320	5	3
9	A-2	260	11	2
10	A-3	250	13	3
11	A-4	275	10	1
12	B-4	255	12	0
13	A-5	300	6	7
14	B-5	190	18	4
15	B-6	240	14	1
16	C-5	200	17	1
17	B-7	210	15	2
18	A-6	165	23	5
19	C-6	185	19	0
20	B-8	180	20	0
21	A-7	175	21	0
22	C-7	170	22	0
23	C-8	205	16	7
Total		$5,880		48

the development of a performance pattern showing where the strongest people are employed. The pattern may indicate where the most challenging work objectives should be assigned.

With this in-depth process, only one reevaluation step is usually necessary to produce a reasonable consensus from which to proceed. Of course, if significant disagreement remains, a third round of ratings is required. In addition, further definition of evaluation criteria may be appropriate.

SALARY RANKING

As a final step, the current salary and salary rank for each employee are added to the group value rating so that the value rating (column 1, Table 12-2) and salary rank (column 4, Table 12-2) can be compared. The arithmetic differences, without regard to sign, are entered in column 5. The total of column 5 in our example is 48. If every employee were paid in direct relation to his value to the organization, the total would be zero.

This information adds a vital dimension to salary reviews. One of the objectives of most salary review systems is to improve the correlation between value rating and salary rank. Success in accomplishing this objective will be reflected in a reduction in the total absolute variance (column 5, Table 12-2). Because of normal attrition and employee turnover, as well as policy limits on salary adjustments, it is virtually impossible to reduce the total to zero. However, any movement in that direction is a measure of improvement.

In our example, an effort has been made to achieve improvement by budgeting all salary adjustments at the beginning of the year. (See Table 12-3.) This budget will not deter supervisors from making modifications as needed during the year to recognize changes in individual performance.

There are dollar limits to the salary increases that can be made. The example assumes an overall salary increase guideline of 5.5 percent of the salary base (column 2, Table 12-3). This provides a budget limit of $323 in increases, to be apportioned among the 23 listed employees. A second assumption is that the maximum annual salary increase allowed by company policy is 15 percent.

SALARY ADJUSTMENTS

Decisions about individual salary adjustments begin with those showing the largest variances in the value/reward comparison (column 5, Table 12-2). The toughest problem is employee A-5, who is ranked sixth in salary but thirteenth in value. By our appraisal, his present job duties are not significant enough to jus-

Table 12-3. Salary plans.

Employee (1)	Present Weekly Salary (2)	Planned Salary Increase (3)	Planned Salary (4)	Planned Salary Rank (5)
A-1	$ 400	$ 30	$ 430	1
C-2	360	16	376	2
B-2	340	16	356	4
C-1	325	32	357	3
B-3	320	0	320	6
A-5	300	−17	283	10
C-3	300	20	320	7
B-1	295	41	336	5
C-4	280	19	299	8
A-4	275	12	287	9
A-2	260	18	278	11
B-4	255	12	267	13
A-3	250	18	268	12
B-6	240	10	250	14
B-7	210	8	218	15
C-8	205	0	205	18
C-5	200	10	210	16
B-5	190	19	209	17
C-6	185	10	195	19
B-8	180	8	188	21
A-7	175	8	183	22
C-7	170	8	178	23
A-6	165	25	190	20
	$5,880	$323	$6,203	

tify a salary of $300 a week—a figure based on his previous responsibilities as a manager. His reassignment to a lower-rated position called for a salary reduction, but it was never made. To correct that oversight, a negative salary adjustment of $17 is planned.

For his current output, C-8 also appears overpaid in his salary range. He is a promising new employee who was recruited at this rate. He has demonstrated management potential by making effective presentations and exercising sound judgment. His suggestions have improved department productivity. No adjustment to his salary is planned this year. He is expected to grow up to it during the year.

A-6 is making maximum effort and is showing outstanding progress. He is outperforming all others in his salary range. As a reward, his salary will be increased by the maximum allowed under company policy. Similarly, a $41 increase is planned for B-1, a $19 increase for B-5, and so on, as shown in column 3 of Table 12-3.

In Table 12-4, the ranking of final planned salaries is compared with the value ratings, and a new absolute variance column is calculated. The planned adjustments have reduced the total variance to 34—a significant improvement over the beginning variance of 48. (Note: In practice, we might rework the adjustments to reduce the variance still more.)

The data in Table 12-3 can also be depicted graphically, as shown in Figure 12-1. Weekly salaries are plotted on a bar graph in descending value ranking, giving a quick visual comparison of how individual salaries relate to value ratings—both before and after planned adjustments.

The chart has been amplified with some background information. The individuals identified with an (S) have previously held supervisory or managerial positions with the company. Although they have been moved into nonsupervisory positions, their salaries have not been adjusted. The problems this situation can create for both the employee and his supervisor often call for special attention and skill. Resolution can be difficult.

The individuals marked (L) have over 15 years of service with the company. Their salaries have increased regularly over this period. As a result of turnover and attrition, the salaries of the newer employees are at market levels. To stay profitable, a company must remain competitive on salaries. Does your salary review system guard against the possibility of increasing salaries above the competitive market?

Employees identified with an (N) are new, less than one year with the group. Naturally, as they become more familiar with their assignments, duties, and responsibilities, their value ratings can be expected to progress. It would be arbitrary and un-

Table 12-4. Comparison of salary rank and value rating.

From Table 12-2		From Table 12-3	Absolute Variance
Group Value Rating (1)	Employee (2)	Group Salary Rank (3)	(1)–(3) (4)
1	A-1	1	0
2	C-1	3	1
3	C-2	2	1
4	B-1	5	1
5	B-2	4	1
6	C-3	7	1
7	C-4	8	1
8	B-3	6	2
9	A-2	11	2
10	A-3	12	2
11	A-4	9	2
12	B-4	13	1
13	A-5	10	3
14	B-5	17	3
15	B-6	14	1
16	C-5	16	0
17	B-7	15	2
18	A-6	20	2
19	C-6	19	0
20	B-8	21	1
21	A-7	22	1
22	C-7	23	1
23	C-8	18	5
Total			34

Figure 12-1. Comparison of employee salaries in dollars per week.

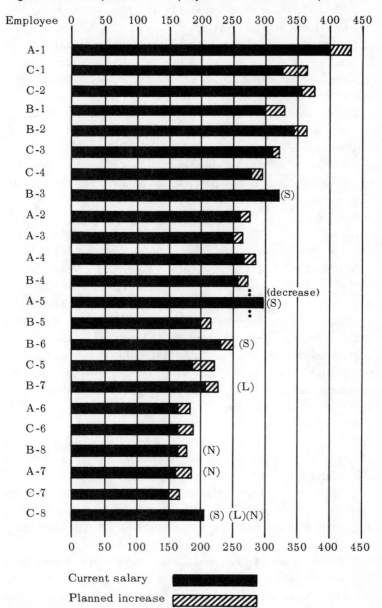

fair to adjust their salaries solely on the basis of their present low level of output. They should be regarded as exceptions for this individual appraisal system.

A further refinement to Table 12-3 is found in Figure 12-2. It is similar to Figure 12-1 except that performance differential is indicated by the amount of space between the horizontal entries. For example, A-1 is more superior to C-1 than C-1 is to C-2. Each employee is rated on a 100-point scale. This is one logical way to quantify value ratings to allow measurement of performance differentials.

For those who wish to add statistical precision to this graphic representation, a best-fit curve applied to these values will provide visual comparison with a smooth curve. This serves as another guide for evaluating salary distribution. The best-fit curve, determined by the least-squares method, for the *present* salary values in our example is plotted in Figure 12-2 to highlight instances of critical deviation. This analysis reinforces assigning first-priority status to the planned reduction in employee A-5's salary. Performing the same analysis on the resultant salary values and comparing the correlation coefficients of the two curves gives another measure of the overall effect of our planned adjustments. In this case, correlation improves from 90 percent for present salary data to 96 percent after planned adjustments, assuming that simple ranking is used without "percentage" ratings.

In the interaction of supervisors, ratings, and policies, you can expect to see more interesting possibilities. Thus an employee who is improving in his job performance may actually fall behind others who are improving faster. Or the departure of a highly rated employee prior to his salary review may result in an excess of planned funds. The introduction of a new supervisor may produce a different value ranking for the same group of individuals.

In our example, we assumed that salary planning is done once a year. This, of course, is a minimum. More frequent modifications to the salary plan enhance its sensitivity to changes in the

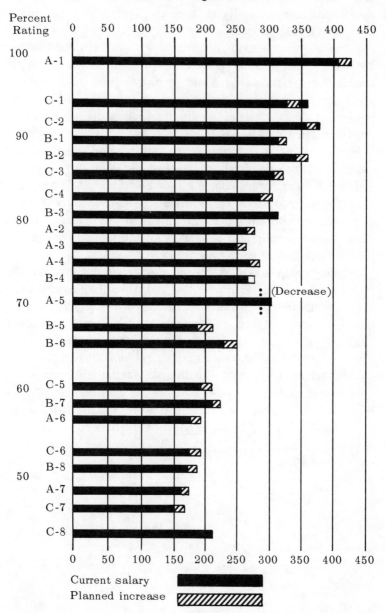

Figure 12-2. Comparison of employee salaries adjusted
for value to organization.

makeup of the group, changes in employee performance, and changes in company policies. To be truly effective in creating a salary structure that fairly rewards employees, salary planning must be a dynamic process.

From the viewpoint of financial analysis, the value ranking approach seems to make sense. Those contributing more to the success of the company should receive higher compensation. (We are not considering nonsalary compensation here.) And budgeting salary changes within the framework of what the company can afford to pay is a sign of practical management.

Bear in mind that financial analysts regularly analyze and compare a firm's financial results. It should come as no surprise to learn that employees compare how they are doing financially too. The most obvious performance comparison an employee can make is within his work group. With this frame of reference, wouldn't he expect a salary structure that corresponds to performance comparisons? Shouldn't you too?

In many companies a central salary review group provides the companywide policies, procedures, and counseling needed to fit departmental objectives into overall company objectives and industry standards. If you are fortunate enough to have specialists available, get them involved in your salary planning process. Their advice, added to your measurement tools (used in the systematic manner described), should give you the information you need to make salary and value coincide for your organization. In this way you can help your company distribute the proceeds of its employees' efforts by paying them what they're worth.

13

Duplication Costs You Plenty

This chapter is not a debate about the relative costs of making electrostatic versus carbon copies. Nor is it an enumeration of reasons to cut down on report distribution lists. It is a discussion of a supervisory bugaboo called "duplication of effort." With a little work, you can find and analyze overlapping work efforts and decide whether they should be continued or eliminated.

Does any duplication of effort take place in your department? Of course it does. Duplication takes place in hundreds of ways. For example:

- When your secretary types your correspondence.
- When you direct subordinates to complete work assignments specified by your boss (or someone else).
- When corrections are required to previously issued reports (or products must be reworked).
- When product packaging is redesigned.
- When you are checking the quality or accuracy of subordinates' work.

Nearly every job assignment has the potential to be duplicated at least once. Thus duplication is a real threat to every aspect of

Portions of this chapter are reprinted, with permission, from *CGA* magazine, December 1977, published by the Canadian Certified General Accountants' Association. © 1977.

your department's work. Supervisors must constantly be alert to stop unnecessary duplication. Success means reduced costs and increased efficiency. Bear in mind that duplication can be good or bad. You are the person to make that distinction.

The story goes that an enemy spy was concealed in a dark corner room in our national capital. He spent months examining Washington at work. At the end of his assignment he told his superior that it was no use bombing the city. He claimed that if one building were destroyed, nothing meaningful would be achieved. Why? His report concluded: "They have two other mirror-image buildings already completely staffed doing exactly the same job. Better to let them confuse themselves in their own bureaucracy."

Perhaps a more peaceful definition of duplication of effort will help you focus on your problem. In this chapter, duplication will mean two or more people (departments, task forces, or other groups) having the same objective and performing the same process on the same data in the same time frame.

Finding and eliminating wasteful duplication is harder than it sounds. Duplication dons many disguises to fool the inattentive or unwary supervisor. And nonduplication efforts (or lack of effort) are often mistaken for them. Do not confuse idleness (waiting for work), a state of no activity, with the active state of duplicating effort.

UNAVOIDABLE DUPLICATION

Sometimes overlaps in work efforts are unavoidable—and necessary—and are not really duplication. Nonduplication efforts that are often perceived to be duplication include:

Team efforts. In this case specialized, balanced input is required for a full response to some outside stimuli. These may include proposal preparation, product development, marketing campaigns, and capital investment decisions.

Customer interfaces. Figure 13-1 identifies several potential interfaces that always exist between your company and its cus-

Figure 13-1. Duplicated customer interfaces.

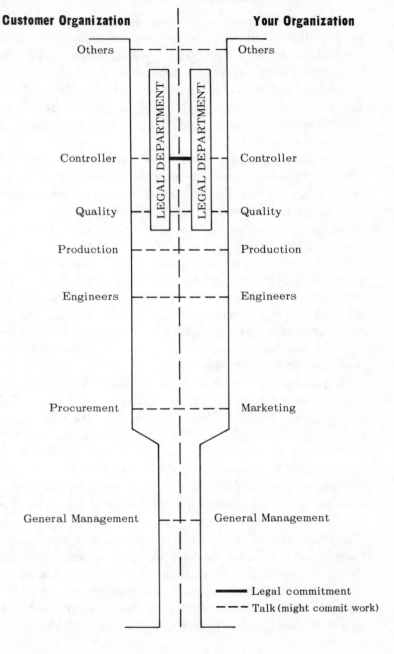

tomers. Each group may make verbal commitments that require work that is not included in the contract terms. Thus if the single legal communication link is not scrupulously followed, expensive problems other than duplication can result.

Creators and users. One group generates data for another to use. For example, design engineering versus production—both need the drawings, and any updates too, if the final product is to work as expected.

Sometimes duplicative effort can be a deliberate reaction to a problem. How many times has a computer system breakdown—inputs that didn't take or printouts that were wrong—delayed your department and caused people to be idle? Result: You can await the rerun, or you can meet your schedule by preparing a manual report (ultimately duplicated by the computer).

There are other complicating situations. Preparers and users of output (data or products) are often independent. Thus an output (data or product) gets manipulated and modified—but for different people and reasons. The same data can provide different answers or generate variable interpretations. The first person with the information can create some critical problems—depending on how it is presented.

How many times have you told management "good" news only to find that someone else has beaten you to the boss? The status-seeking duplicate takes credit for the work you've done and makes your routine functional organization look slow in the process. An analogy can be found in the TV nightly news. Radio and daily newspapers are doing essentially the same job. Because they stress different aspects of the same story, they seem to be doing independent jobs. But it's duplication. They don't create the news events.

In a large factory or office it is more difficult for management to recognize that the person doing the reporting didn't necessarily do any productive work. Result: When *all* the "news" is issued (the completed routine report is received and filed), it is discredited for being slow, inadequate, or unsatisfying to the recipient. It's up to the supervisor to avoid this situation.

A financial reports supervisor received the following rebuke from an operations vice president:

> Thank you for the timely financial reports sent to me for April 197X. Their format is excellent for my use and, I hope, for my staff. However, I need some additional information, starting with the May results. Like how are we doing against budget? In addition to the numbers, I need some prose that answers the question "Why?" Some typical questions from month to month include: (1) Why do costs exceed latest plan? (2) Why has "latest plan" been changed? Also, on the Allocation Pool Spending Analysis, I need some prose or a further breakdown (or both) of the "controllable" account. What bothered me most on the Allocation Pool Analysis was the fact that our actual costs exceeded plan and yet we are 28 people *understaffed*. Should this bother me?
>
> In summary, the report format is outstanding for my use. However, I already have the news. All you issue are reports, not analyses. I need the analyses by your experts to save me time in follow-up. When will you give me what I want?

Of course, the desired analysis delays the report a few days—and the vice president won't understand additional delay unless you point out why it is necessary.

In this example, the supervisor has at least been put on notice that the vice president is unhappy. But what else has happened? A special analysis must be created—or else. In addition, the managers reporting to the vice president need a special analysis to protect themselves from the vice president's special analysis (and questions it may generate). And so on down the line. The financial supervisor and his staff now become known as "spies." They must try to pry out answers to questions the vice president may ask. The likely result is that this supervisor will be labeled the "VP's snoop," and the data required will probably be withheld from him, making him look less competent than before. Although this duplication of effort was designed by top management to help it manage the business, the result may turn out to be a multilevel game of hide-and-seek. The problem is that no one really wins the contest.

This example illustrates a facet of duplication that further increases its costs. Some duplication is required. Demands for reporting are issued by local management, headquarters staff (if your firm has more than one location), customers, and the various federal, state, and local regulatory agencies. To be sure the "right" information is issued, a second analysis cycle may be initiated. This type of duplication is found in:

1. Program reviews
   a. Schedules met and missed
   b. Comparisons of performance against cost targets or spending plans
   c. Systems shipped
2. Financial reviews
   a. IRS or SEC requirements
   b. Internal goal achievement measurements
   c. Government contract requirements
   d. Insurance value reports
3. Personnel (headcount) recaps
   a. Breakdowns by department, sex, nationality, position grades, pay rates
   b. Summary data by plant location
   c. Summary data by operating divisions or wholly owned subsidiaries

Note that in these examples the duplication is required by someone over whom the local supervisor has little control. The control of outside agencies seems to be someone else's job— and that's one reason why duplication flourishes.

Consider the work of a typical audit staff. It reviews the work done by personnel, engineering, production control, and administration. The review is a duplication that leads to more duplication. Here is an excerpt from a fairly typical audit report:

> It is our opinion that the billing function at location X has stabilized and can be relied upon to generate reliable financial information in all material respects.

This statement was followed by a nine-page report covering ten separate subjects. The report was submitted to 14 executives. This company's policy requires that a formal response be filed to an audit report. Thus 15 (auditor plus 14) follow-up files are created—to receive a response that said:

> We believe our corrective actions have been effective and are confident we are adhering to policy. It is suggested that a follow-up audit be made to verify this.

The final payoff: *a duplicate audit.*

It doesn't have to be this way. Years ago I worked with a data processing supervisor who refused to use his programmers, systems analysts, operators, or computer for any application that didn't generate at least four by-product uses. He rejected all single-purpose applications. This requirement forced his organization to do considerable thinking and organizing before committing resources. He fought duplication and built an extremely efficient network of user systems. It was a tough uphill battle, but he won the respect of management.

Unfortunately, not every organization has someone so committed to fighting "required" duplication. Another data processing supervisor I know accepts every service request he receives. He has successfully fought off the establishment of a user board aimed at controlling computer usage. Result: He has increased his hardware complex 400 percent in the past five years. During the same period his company's sales volume has increased only 60 percent.

AVOIDABLE DUPLICATION

Up to now we've limited the discussion to required duplication of efforts. Unrequired and avoidable duplication also occurs. Nine causes are fairly typical. They can be divided into two groups: deliberate and accidental. The list below may help you see if any are present in your department.

DELIBERATE CAUSES

Failure to trust someone else's work.

A self-assured insistence on "doing it myself."

An attempt to find the "best" answer (that is, the answer that makes me look best.

ACCIDENTAL CAUSES

Subordinates unconsciously doing more than required.

Vague job descriptions (or none at all).

Salvaging product spoiled in processing.

Mistaken task assignments.

Competition.

Pride.

Elimination of the deliberate causes requires that everyone be directed to consistently find and use one source of information. In today's interrelated business environment this may be impossible, since most managers want the power early information gives them. In addition, egos can be a problem. A few supervisors deliberately use their staff to advance their career without regard to the good of the company. No one is safe around the egotist who must (1) be first to develop the "miracle" product; (2) always be a hero; (3) find data to destroy the credibility of a peer; or (4) spend "common" money before anyone else can. Such a supervisor will often keep triple sets of books to report to customers, local management, and headquarters staff. (This problem inevitably leads to others, including excess costs, tax problems, and personal rivalries.)

Withdrawal is the opposite: that is, a supervisor who isn't satisfied when the problem is solved. He requires extra work to justify why his being number 2 is O.K., saying that "Losing was good, because . . ." or "The competition was wired to win this one."

The frustrated supervisor can also create duplication problems. When a supervisor proclaims, "I don't understand how this could happen," "I'm not convinced you've done everything," or "You're not supporting me," someone will have to do extra work to overcome this feeling of insecurity. Often, the supervisor's frustration is due to his failure to specify a work assignment adequately. The supervisor does not know exactly what he wants, is fishing for something else, or is simply confused. To avoid appearing ignorant, he directs the work effort to begin without doing needed research. Then after his staff makes numerous unsuccessful attempts to "solve the problem," he gets angry. The supervisor scolds the doers, totally missing the point that he's the one responsible.

To eliminate the accidental causes of duplication, departmental or divisional charters must be defined with related task assignments carefully spelled out *and agreed to*. The benefits are well worth the cost. If duplication is the result of enthusiastic, dedicated workers—that is, if subordinates achieve more than they are asked—try to rechannel their efforts to other assignments. Do not be critical.

Ask your staff about other ways to eliminate duplication. Do they perceive any duplication of effort? It's easy to find out. Figure 13-2 is a simple questionnaire. Distribute it and ask for anonymous replies. Maybe you won't get any answers. But one positive finding, a single improvement in your department's workload, will soon lead to another.

Make sure your staff realizes that repeated consolidation of data is duplicative. Note the substantial expense to:

Report by supervisor (or work station)
Roll it up to manager
Roll it up to vice president
Roll it up to president
Roll it up to final corporate summary

Consolidating data for government and management (to use or not to use) is expensive. The government's regulations are law; management's are discretionary. If you ask for something, be clear. Get it, then use it!

Every work effort has a customer. It is essential to find out what your customer really wants. Let him know what he really

Figure 13-2. Duplication-of-effort questionnaire.

To: Staff members

From: Your Supervisor
Department: Ours
Subject: Survey of Duplication
of Effort

I need your help. I'm concerned that we are doing more work than we have to. Please answer the following questions and return this question-naire to me by _____.

1. Do you think there is anyone in our department duplicating any part of your job function?
   If you answer "yes," please indicate the duplication of effort.
   Do you have any ideas on what we can do to change it?

2. Do you feel there is anyone elsewhere in the company whose work you are duplicating?
   If you answer "yes," please indicate the duplication of effort.
   Do you have any ideas on what we can do to change it?

is getting. Decisions on when and how he will get it and how much he must pay for it also require early resolution.

Have you noticed that many causes of duplication are related to the supervisor? Perhaps the solution to a duplication-of-effort problem is to better train and discipline supervisors. It's ironic, but supervisory situational training involves duplication and repetition too as major elements of the learning process.

HOW MUCH DUPLICATION IS NECESSARY?

How much duplication does management want? One simple fact stands out. Management directs supervisors. Supervisors direct the working troops. These troops do duplication. Some duplication is bad. Is it reasonable to conclude that management ordered bad duplication? Can the supervisor do something about it? Perhaps management can be shocked into corrective action.

The president of an electricity-generating company was electrocuted in the main generator room of his plant. His VP called the sheriff and the coroner, and gathered the firm's supervisors together. They stood in disbelief around the body of the dead man. The coroner began to speculate on how such an experienced man could commit such a fatal error. "The only thing I can think of," said the supervisor of the main generator room, "is that Mr. Jones must have picked up the blue terminal with one hand." The supervisor then picked up the terminal and without thinking reached out with his other hand and touched it. Bingo! The supervisor was dead. The supervisor's actions solved the mystery to everyone's satisfaction.

Duplication may not be so easy to clarify or so deadly in your situation, but the results can be as electrifying. Your efforts to reduce unnecessary duplication should be a daily priority item. But be careful. Establish objectives clearly. Compare. Evaluate. Find the unnecessary duplication, and eliminate it. As you do, you will make time available for new duties, thus reducing your cost of operations and helping your supervisory career.

14

Evaluate Human Resources Requirements

It is a rare supervisor who will admit he has too many employees. In fact, most complain they never have enough of the right kind of help. Their problem is that they always have too much work. Inadequate staffing is an excuse commonly used to extend due dates, explain delays, and refuse work. There are other aspects to staffing problems too. One is found whenever a staff is composed of stagnant, obsolete people, subordinates who apparently have lost interest in their work and have nowhere to go. A second is seen in the rapidly expanding growth company, where promotions occur with blinding speed.

A third problem occurs when there is a sudden change in the economy. For instance, have you ever been surprised by a sudden shift in demand for your products or services? Were you able to respond quickly enough to satisfy your bosses, subordinates, customers, and stockholders? Were you able to staff up or down smoothly, without creating a whole host of people problems? Have you ever come to the end of a product life (or a production run) and wondered what to do with the people producing that product? How do you handle the staffing problems created by a contract termination?

Adapted, by permission of the publisher, from *Advanced Management Journal*, Winter 1977. © 1977 by S.A.M., a division of American Management Associations. All rights reserved.

Have you identified the staffing levels, education, and skills required in your department for the next 6, 12, 24, 36, or 60 months? Have you determined the functional mix of people necessary to meet ever changing company objectives and government regulations? Have you evaluated work output trends? When was the last time you correlated a current workforce analysis with a detailed projection of anticipated manpower requirements? Although all these issues sound very difficult, costly, and time-consuming, they don't have to be. Every time someone assigns work to your department, you get involved in several of these activities. As you decide to accept or reject work, you are consciously or unconsciously applying elements of manpower planning.

HUMAN RESOURCES PLANNING SYSTEMS

What does human resources planning mean? There is no consensus. When you put this question to supervisors in the production, quality control, engineering, program management, personnel, marketing and controller's departments, you'll seldom get total agreement on an answer. The supervisors in the controller's department may say, "Human resources planning is the process used to determine labor costs in developing the budgets for product cost and overhead rates." Marketing may respond, "It's the number of people we need to cover the territory." Personnel may say, "It's the number of people required to fulfill the people needs of the other groups." Engineering will say, "It's the skills we need to solve the technical problems in house today, plus skills needed to research the technology to design and develop new products for tomorrow." Production suggests, "It's the people we need to keep the assembly lines rolling." By combining these general answers, we get a definition along these lines: "Human resources planning is the process of determining where and when skilled people are needed, at a cost that allows the enterprise to continue for a specified time period."

But is that the total answer? Is it possible to get a more practical one—an answer that is good for more than today? I don't think so. Because of changing regulations, marketing opportunities, technological advances, improved production processes, and personnel turnover, a practical answer today will have to be changed tomorrow—and again the day after. I contend that we must have a management definition to develop a manageable human resources planning baseline. This baseline can be fixed or flexible. But it must be used to direct marketing and personnel efforts. As these departments become synchronized, the engineering, production, quality control, and controller's departments can be planned more effectively and utilized more efficiently. As a supervisor integrated into a human resources planning system, you have a choice of short-run alternatives and can be alerted to the potential of long-run changes.

A human resources planning system may take several forms. Supervisor A has no system at all. Whenever a "need" develops, he hires someone. The reaction system assumes that a qualified person is available at an acceptable cost and can become instantly productive. Each department or function of the company operates independently by the "seat of its pants." This system works fairly well for low-skill, entry-level clerical, maintenance, service, and production positions.

Supervisor B uses a "requirements forecasting" approach. Each worker is asked to produce data on the number of hours needed to meet known job objectives and production schedules. This is generally a short-term system that assumes continuation of a highly predictable employment market and a customer base for some predetermined time period. Such a system may be found on a process flow construction contract or in a job shop environment. The system is plagued with layoffs, rehires, and other abrupt personnel changes.

Supervisor C defines tomorrow's needs in relation to today's workforce. He requires trend analysis and close coordination of all company functions. Human resources are inventoried and changes in market or product mix are forecast. Sales strategies, hiring and training programs, and production processes are coordinated to take best advantage of market opportunities. He is always alert for potential replacements in other departments, at the club—wherever they might be available. I call this the "personnel requirements outline," or PRO system. It requires an evaluation process that could be the key to solving your most difficult human resources problems.

An interesting parallel to the PRO system exists in professional football. Injuries and retirements affect key people. The product changes. Offenses and defenses come and go. The rules of the game change. Yet some teams win consistently. The winners adjust best because they follow a personnel requirements outline. Of course, their needs are usually well defined. They need 11 people playing known positions on the field when the ball is in play. So how do they staff it? First they scout available talent. Then they hold tryouts at the position they need filled. Each position is expected to perform specific assignments on every play. Each player is filmed, studied, charted, and graded. The skills required for each position are carefully developed through training and practice. When a team has successfully scouted, drafted, evaluated, and developed its personnel, it has championship potential. Add coaching and leadership and the team is Super Bowl bound.

Human resources planning is necessary whether you have 5, 11, 22, or 1,000 positions to fill. Your department can build championship potential with a PRO system. Unfortunately, you don't have the benefit of instant replay or game films to run and rerun. Your system must be comprehensive, yet simple and easy to use. Your PRO system will be based on complete knowledge of *what's happening to the workforce you have*. Because this vital step is frequently overlooked in human resources planning, the following sections will zero in on developing the personnel profiles of your department or company today.

DEVELOPING PERSONNEL PROFILES

The first step in developing personnel profiles is to maintain basic personnel data about your staff. You need to know the hire date, salary, age, job classification, date of last salary action, supervisory evaluation, date and kind of last degree, and continuing education program for each professional employee. You should create profiles for positions presently unfilled. (Don't overlook supervisory personnel in this survey.) Thoughtful analysis of the data will show you what to scout for.

When the data are summarized, they should indicate trends that will show you areas that require attention. (It's better to find out now than later, through loss of people, products, or market share.) The data will also identify weaknesses (an accounting department with no trained accountants) and strengths (a marketing organization that has significant background in production and engineering).

The illustrations that follow will assume that basic personnel data are available for the past two years. Granted, two years is a minimum for finding a trend, but it will give you a chance to organize data, set a baseline, and send out scouts. If you have no data available, start now to build your data base. Interview incumbents—beside helping you get data they'll probably enjoy the attention.

We will examine a company that has grown overall from 500 employees to 750. Assume it has five main departments: production, engineering, personnel, marketing, and controller. Assume further that it has seven categories of employees: managerial, supervisory, administrative, sales, technical, clerical, and production. These general classifications are arbitrary, and their definitions depend on the nature of your business.

From the basic personnel data, seven key analyses can be made to indicate potential problem areas. Repeating the analyses at regular intervals adds precision to the human resources evaluation process.

Table 14-1 illustrates how average age and length of service have changed for managers in each department. Such a survey might indicate that an age gap exists between functions or within a function. If so, it could be the reason for a communication breakdown. Broadened into other classifications, it may indicate that a pool of potential supervisors exists in one of the nonmanagement classifications.

Table 14-1. Average length of service of managers, by age group.

Department	Under 30 No.	Under 30 Length Service	30–39 No.	30–39 Length Service	40–49 No.	40–49 Length Service	50–59 No.	50–59 Length Service	60 and Over No.	60 and Over Length Service
1977										
Controller	0	0	1	6	1	10	1	15	1	20
Engineering	1	5	9	10	2	15	2	13	0	0
Marketing	4	3	2	5	0	0	0	0	0	0
Personnel	0	0	1	4	1	8	1	15	1	17
Production	2	4	10	8	4	11	4	12	2	14
Total	7	3	23	8	8	12	8	13	4	16
1978										
Controller	0	0	1	7	2	8	1	16	1	20
Engineering	2	6	7	12	3	11	3	9	1	17
Marketing	4	4	2	6	0	0	0	0	0	0
Personnel	0	0	2	5	1	9	1	16	1	18
Production	4	4	14	7	4	12	4	13	2	15
Total	10	4	26	8	10	11	9	12	5	17
1979										
Controller	0	0	1	8	2	9	1	17	1	21
Engineering	1	5	8	13	2	14	3	10	2	19
Marketing	4	2	3	1	0	0	0	0	0	0
Personnel	0	0	3	8	1	10	1	17	1	19
Production	5	5	18	8	5	13	5	14	3	16
Total	10	4	33	9	10	12	10	13	7	18

Several "what if" questions are suggested by this survey. For instance: What if management has aged two years in two years' time? Is it getting stale? Does this indicate that you should "draft" or train some new talent? New ideas may not readily gain acceptance in an atmosphere of aging management. Perhaps you should push for a forced attrition program. On the other hand, you may volunteer to take on more (or new) assignments, thus proving you are ready to step up.

Other "what if" questions can be raised. What if youthful engineers are wasting resources on pet projects that have little profit potential? What if no one under 30 is a manager? What if all clerical personnel are under 25? (Personnel profiles bring such condiitons to light so you can evaluate their potential impact on your organization.) What if no staffer ever stays past one year? Are you wasting training dollars? Is the selection process deficient? Are you a poor supervisor? Are your pay policies inadequate?

The salary analysis for our hypothetical company in Table 14-2 indicates a regressive salary policy. Employees with greater length of service are receiving progressively smaller percentage increases. The payment interval is being stretched out too. While this may signify that older employees are "topping out," it could also warn of morale problems among older professional workers. The situation raises some serious questions. Is your salary program acting as an incentive? Are individuals being rewarded in relation to contribution? What is the risk that you will lose key people? Will you develop a group of hangers-on by accident? Will these hangers-on then be promoted by default—because everyone else has left? Perhaps you should re-examine your policy on giving pay raises.

Table 14-3 analyzes employee turnover—a supervisory concern that has the potential to make or lose a lot of money. Unplanned turnover wastes manpower resources at all levels. If your firm promotes from within, the loss of one person could generate a number of changes. The cost-benefit relationship is hard to evaluate. Departments with very high turnover can give the appearance of efficiently operating within dollar budgets because most of the salaries are near the entry-level (lowest) rate. Lowest doesn't automatically mean cheapest or most efficient. Could efficiency be improved by paying more to fewer employees? Would this improve the quality of the staff and the product or service? Use your employment application form to create a profile of answers you want from applicants. Compare new applicants' answers with those given by productive, long-service employees. Hire people who best match the desired

Table 14-2. Salary increase analysis.

	Supervisors			Clerical Employees		
	Merit	Promotion	Merit Promotion	Merit	Promotion	Merit Promotion
Average dollar increase	$26.20	$28.80	$26.90	$13.10	$18.00	$14.50
Average percent increase	8.6%	10.3%	9.1%	7.8%	11.0%	8.7%
Average years of service	10.4	8.6	10.0	6.8	6.5	6.7
Average months between increases	14.3	12.3	13.8	10.0	10.8	10.2

Table 14-3. Employee turnover
(figures rounded to nearest percent).

Personnel Classification	Average Manpower			Terminations			Turnover Rate		
	1977	1978	1979	1977	1978	1979	1977	1978	1979
Managerial	50	60	70	2	3	4	4%	5%	6%
Supervisory	10	12	15	1	1	5	10	8	33
Administrative	20	36	55	10	10	45	50	28	82
Sales	20	22	25	5	2	0	20	9	0
Technical	60	70	80	30	35	20	50	50	25
Clerical	40	50	70	40	50	35	100	100	50
Production	300	350	435	100	100	150	33	29	34
	500	600	750	188	201	259	38%	35%	35%

answers. This will increase the likelihood of selecting satisfactory employees—and can reduce the turnover rate too.

In our hypothetical example, turnover rates are relatively stable. However, a close look at specific classifications raises several questions. Why are supervisory and administrative turnover rates up? Why are technical and clerical rates down? Did policies change? Did the expected result occur? Did the selection process change? Can the turnover be related to length of service? Can the production department afford that high turnover? What would a 5 percent reduction in turnover be worth in increased profits? As a supervisor in the production department, you could improve your chances for promotion by answering these questions.

Employees approaching retirement age should be regularly identified (see Table 14-4), and their individual value to the organization should be determined. In our example, when Mr. Grant or Ms. Harris leaves, Product B production management will be wiped out. If you recognize such a situation early, you'll have time to develop adequate replacements. If you wait, the productivity loss may be extensive.

The salary distribution shown in Table 14-5 can easily be compiled for your department. It shows how rising labor costs can be a significant factor in marketing decisions. If turnover is not controlled and costs are creeping up it would be disastrous to have marketing convert its energy to implementing a price competition strategy. Evaluate your labor cost trend and relate it to productivity measures. You may find that a planned turnover

Table 14-4. Potential retirees.

Name	Department	Category	Retirement Date Normal	Retirement Date Early	Special Skill
Smith, A. W.	Controller	Manager	1980	1979	Yes
Jones, E. B.	Engineering	Technical	1980	1979	No
Olson, U. U.	Personnel	Administrative	1981	1979	Yes
Grant, Y. N.	Production	Manager	1981	1980	Yes
Harris, M. N.	Production	Manager	1982	1979	Yes

Table 14-5. Salary distribution for engineering function.

Salary Range	Production			Clerical			Administrative			Technical			Supervisory			Management		
	1977	1978	1979	1977	1978	1979	1977	1978	1979	1977	1978	1979	1977	1978	1979	1977	1978	1979
Under 5,000	1	0	1	2	3	3	0	0	0	0	0	0	0	0	0	0	0	0
5–7,500	12	13	15	7	8	10	0	0	0	0	0	0	0	0	0	0	0	0
7,500–10,000	2	7	9	1	1	1	2	3	7	40	35	30	2	2	2	0	0	0
10–12,500	0	0	0	0	0	1	3	4	6	0	0	0	0	0	0	0	0	0
12,500–15,000	0	0	0	0	0	0	0	1	1	15	30	35	1	2	2	1	1	1
15–17,500	0	0	0	0	0	0	0	0	1	5	5	10	2	2	3	2	2	2
17,500–20,000	0	0	0	0	0	0	0	0	0	0	0	5	0	0	0	2	2	3
20,000–22,500	0	0	0	0	0	0	0	0	0	0	0	0	0	0	0	2	2	2
22,500–25,000	0	0	0	0	0	0	0	0	0	0	0	0	0	0	0	1	2	2
25,000–27,500	0	0	0	0	0	0	0	0	0	0	0	0	0	0	0	1	1	2
27,500–30,000	0	0	0	0	0	0	0	0	0	0	0	0	0	0	0	1	1	1
Over 30,000	0	0	0	0	0	0	0	0	0	0	0	0	0	0	0	0	1	2
	15	20	25	10	12	15	5	8	15	60	70	80	5	6	7	10	12	15

144   Evaluation Techniques

program is needed. If your trend is toward lower-cost but less efficient personnel, perhaps a higher training budget is required.

Do you know the likelihood that an employee will stay with you from one year to the next? Table 14-6 shows the expected turnover (based on history) of new hires in each year. In this case, 50 percent of this year's new hires will be gone in three years. If an improvement in the selection process could decrease this to 25 percent, you could improve productivity, reduce recruitment and personnel costs. Result: The previously mentioned marketing price competition might be a good strategy. In like manner, if next year 50 percent of new hires leave again in the *first* year, you have warning that a new problem has developed.

Reading from Table 14-6 is quite easy. For example, the probability of an employee with nine years of experience completing the next year is .867. To find this answer, select "To Year" entry 10 and read across to "From Year" column 9. The probability of an employee with 2 years' experience reaching 20 years is only .091.

Table 14-6. Probability of production personnel staying.

To Year	0	1	2	3	4	5	6	7	8	9	10	11	12	13	14	15	16	17	18	19	20
0	1																				
1	.776	1																			
2	.612	.789	1																		
3	.490	.632	.800	1																	
4	.390	.512	.649	.811	1																
5	.326	.420	.533	.666	.821	1															
6	.271	.349	.443	.553	.682	.831	1														
7	.227	.293	.372	.465	.573	.698	.840	1													
8	.193	.249	.316	.394	.487	.593	.713	.849	1												
9	.166	.214	.271	.338	.418	.508	.612	.728	.858	1											
10	.144	.185	.235	.293	.362	.440	.531	.632	.744	.867	1										
11	.126	.162	.206	.256	.317	.385	.465	.553	.651	.759	.875	1									
12	.111	.143	.182	.226	.280	.340	.410	.488	.575	.670	.773	.883	1								
13	.099	.127	.162	.201	.249	.303	.365	.435	.512	.597	.688	.787	.891	1							
14	.099	.115	.146	.181	.224	.272	.328	.391	.460	.537	.619	.707	.801	.899	1						
15	.081	.104	.132	.164	.203	.247	.298	.355	.417	.484	.561	.641	.727	.815	.907	1					
16	.074	.095	.121	.150	.186	.226	.272	.324	.382	.446	.514	.587	.665	.746	.830	.915	1				
17	.068	.088	.111	.138	.171	.208	.251	.299	.352	.411	.474	.541	.613	.688	.765	.844	.922	1			
18	.063	.081	.103	.129	.159	.194	.233	.278	.327	.382	.440	.503	.570	.640	.712	.785	.857	.930	1		
19	.059	.076	.097	.121	.149	.182	.219	.260	.306	.358	.413	.472	.534	.599	.667	.735	.803	.871	.937	1	
20	.056	.072	.091	.114	.141	.172	.106	.245	.289	.338	.389	.446	.504	.566	.629	.694	.758	.823	.885	.944	1

From Year

Table 14-7 shows the educational profile of the company. This could also be prepared by personnel classification or type of degree for your department. In the example 1978 stands out as a year of growth. But 1979 shows a reduction. Since our test company was defined as a growing one, this may indicate a problem. Investigate whether today's jobs are beneath the level required for a degree holder. Perhaps some other breakdown has occurred in the human resources planning process.

PREDICTING HUMAN RESOURCES NEEDS

These surveys demonstrate ways to analyze your human resources inventory. They can tell you where you are now and pinpoint where changes are taking place—that is, where you need a replacement scouting program. But they will not predict the future demand for your products and services. They will not predict exactly what kinds of people you will need tomorrow.

Such predictions require a production and technology forecast. Whether you use a Delphi technique (obtaining the inputs of all your executives), a probabilistic model, a factored marketing forecast, or merely a seat-of-the pants guess, you need help in forecasting people and skill needs. By predicting future demand for new or existing products and services, you can identify the affected labor categories and quantify your needs. Further analysis will help you define skill deficiencies by product and service. Summarizing the data gives you a human resource profile. Compare this with your available people inventory and the variance defines a plan for action. This process should be repeated at regular intervals. *Whenever* an unplanned event occurs, the baseline should be retested and variable data updated.

Your particular type of operation will determine how you define future needs, how you handle recruitment for each new opening, and how you evaluate individual performance. You must compare the training costs for new, entry-level people you may lose against the costs of (1) retraining "obsolete" person-

Table 14-7. Employee educational profile (level achieved and years since degree).

Function	Bachelor's			Master's			Ph.D.		
	Total	> 5 Yrs.	< 5 Yrs.	Total	> 5 Yrs.	< 5 Yrs.	Total	> 5 Yrs.	< 5 Yrs.
Production	7	6	1	1	1	0	1	1	0
Engineering	22	5	17	7	2	5	3	0	3
Personnel	3	3	0	1	1	0	0	0	0
Marketing	5	2	3	1	1	0	0	0	0
Controller	4	3	1	1	1	0	0	0	0
Totals 1979	41	19	22	11	6	5	4	1	3
Totals 1978	49	27	22	13	8	5	4	2	2
Totals 1977	38	22	16	9	6	3	2	1	1

nel and (2) hiring higher-level trained people who can step right into the job as needed.

As you blend your findings with overall market availability, you will find that you can better predict your specific human resources needs. As you master the system, you too will become a supervisory PRO—the kind of PRO who steps up to top management.

15

Stake Out Your Claim on Talent

The word "talent" originally referred to a monetary unit having weight and value. The Hebrew silver talent was valued at 3,000 silver shekels; in Athens, the silver talent was worth slightly less. A golden talent also had different weights and values.

SCOUTING FOR TALENT

Over time, "talent" has come to mean the native ability of an individual to achieve a specific task. It is an ability that can be discovered, shaped, formed, directed, and improved. Even today, talent comes in different shapes and sizes. Yet some supervisors don't seem to believe that.

Today, talent is usually associated with an entertainer or sports hero. Experts skilled in finding these people are called talent scouts. Major Bowes, Arthur Godfrey, and Ted Mack are recognized scouts who found talented entertainers. Most professional sports teams have a nationwide network of scouts. Their job is to locate men and women with the potential to become stars—heroes who will lead their teams to national and international championships. After the talent is found and signed to exclusive contracts, the best teachers and coaches are provided. The individual is finely trained, developed, and publicized. Re-

148

sult: The star is easily recognized. Often, his or her name is exploited for profit.

Our society places a premium on talent. Do you? Have you ever looked for talent resident in your current workforce? Do you prospect for talent the way one accounting supervisor did?

He asked the staff psychologist to judge several applicants for the position of accounting clerk. The choice narrowed down to one of three young women. Each one was asked, "What do 2 and 2 make?"

"It must be 4," replied the first.

"It might be 22," said the second.

"It could be 22 or 4," answered the third.

The psychologist reported that the first woman gave the obvious answer, the second gave a cautious answer, and the third played it both ways. He told the supervisor that the final choice was up to him. "Based on psychological findings, I'll take the second one," said the supervisor, "that lovely blonde with the blue eyes." Is that the way you select people, or do you use some other method to justify your choice?

Have you ever heard of anyone being recognized for finding talented engineers, salesmen, accountants, or supervisors? As we have already seen, finding talent on the job is difficult and demanding. It requires considerable judgment. And supervisors can make the job more difficult by letting their habits, biases, and fears get in the way.

How many notions do you unconsciously accept that restrict your ability to attract and develop talented performers? Let me suggest a few. Do you believe:

9:00 A.M. to 5:00 P.M. is a standard workday?

Five days is a standard workweek?

No public transportation to outlying plant locations is necessary?

A supervisor must be a protective buffer?

"Over 40" is obsolete?

Certain jobs require a bachelor's or a master's degree?

Women have different objectives from men?
Women can't travel overnight?
Women are too emotional?
No one should need a babysitter to work?
Transfers should not be allowed?
A subordinate should never be allowed to work with management?
Successful candidates must have prior experience?
A supervisor should take credit for subordinate's work?
Management makes all the bad decisions?
You should cover up the efforts of subordinates?
Your secretary is to blame for your mistakes (missed appointments or due dates, bad reports, and so on)?
Managers should be rewarded for making profit, not for developing people?
EEO goals are quotas?
Men should be paid more than women?

Innovations in company policies are beginning to overturn some of these beliefs, but acceptance comes very slowly. Changes include workweek compression, job rotation development programs for senior employees, permanent part-time employment, flexible work hours, resident sitter services, employee reevaluations, and company car pools. Supervisory attitudes are also changing. EEO legislation, human rights commissions, and more assertive female workers have brought further changes. Nevertheless, progress is slow. As a supervisor, you can help shape your company's response by developing a sound program for selecting new employees.

SOURCES OF TALENT

People with the talent you need are available from three major sources. As a prospector for talent, you must carefully assess each. The first place to look is local educational institutions. Work-study programs at high schools, colleges, and universities give potential employees a chance to demonstrate their developing talent. As a "forty-niner," are you fully alert to this source?

The University of Minnesota School of Business has a special one-quarter quantitative analysis class for graduate students. Homework assignments are tied to local industry. Profit and nonprofit firms in the community submit real-world problems that face them. Problems are posted for class evaluation and selection. Students sign up for the problem that interests them and are formed into teams of four. The teams work at the firms for ten weeks, gathering data and applying the principles learned in class. Their objective is to generate quantitative solutions. At the end of the quarter they orally present their answers to the class *and* to the management of the firm. Their reward is a grade, class critique, and a chance to practice what they've learned in an on-the-job environment.

Metropolitan State University in St. Paul, Minnesota, has established a series of credit-earning internship programs for its students. The internships, which vary from three months to a year or more, allow students to participate in meaningful work experiences and to gain skills and knowledge related to career goals. Again, the students effectively work part-time for local firms. Each student is supported by a member of the faculty and an internship adviser—often a functional area supervisor. Supervisors believe the program gives them the opportunity to find, develop, and test the talents of potential subordinates.

Are you personally involved with any programs like these? Do any exist in your area? If they do, get involved. They give you an early claim on, and evaluation of, talent.

A second obvious place to "pan" for talent is in the ranks of the temporarily unemployed. Checking this source tests your firm's equal opportunity program and your personal biases too. Here's a test case: Given the chance to hire a 38-year-old retired marine, what talent do you expect to find? According to his résumé, after 20 years of service he has completed one career. He has been stationed all around the world. He had a senior rating. While in the service, he conducted training classes in electronics for recruits and junior-grade officers. He also supervised a number of American citizens and foreign nationals.

He may have a high potential as an overseas branch manager, a training officer, or an electronics technician. Does he automatically get considered for a management slot? He is an individual with special abilities. Will your panning technique identify, and recommend, him for his abilities, or will his application be routinely washed out and sent to the supervisor of building maintenance?

Another type of retiree entering the workforce is the middle-aged housewife whose children have left home. Will your "miners" classify her as employable? In what capacity? Is she classified as clerical or assembly-line material? Her background may include experience as a teacher's aide, Sunday school leader, stringer for the local newspaper, 4-H group leader, or city councilwoman, and may include training at many adult education classes. She's been busy creating public opinion and solving problems at home. She's been leading the community while you've managed your affairs on the job. Will your prospectors recognize her organizational strengths and put them to work?

A third source of talent, in addition to the rich lodes listed above, are employees already at work in your organization. They must be assayed too. People currently on the payroll should be scouted first. Don't automatically write someone off on hearsay or another supervisor's experience. It may be invalid. How can you find talent in house? One way to locate resident talent is to establish a policy requiring internal advertising of job openings. Given high visibility, it encourages people already employed to apply for better jobs.

In response to demands from its supervisors, a midwestern firm requires that all job openings below manager level be posted on a bulletin board for one week before outside candidates are interviewed. (See Figure 15-1.) Interested employees need only complete an application form, as shown in Figure 15-2A. The reverse side of the form is shown as Figure 15-2B.

The program also requires that all applicants be interviewed by the posting supervisor. Interview decisions are fed back to the applicants. Unsuccessful applicants are briefed on why they didn't win the job and on what is needed to win. In this way "losers" are winners too, since they learn what is required for

Figure 15-1. Job posting form.

An Internal Advancement Opportunity

Posting Period: Week of _____ to _____

Job   Job   Exempt/Nonexempt/
Classification _____ Title _____ Hourly _____

Job
Grade _____ Shift____ Location_____

Salary Range (weekly)   Minimum_____ Maximum _____

Requesting Organization_____ Requesting Supervisor_____

Description of work _____

_____

_____

_____

_____

Suggested applicant qualifications (education and experience)_____

_____

_____

_____

_____

To apply for this position, complete an "I want an Internal Advancement Opportunity" form and send it to personnel. Keep a copy for your files.

Figure 15-2A. Application form for internal advancement (front).

I Want an Internal Advancement Opportunity

Employee _____ Date Submitted_____

Current   Mail   Telephone   Home
Organization _____ Station _____ ext. _____ phone _____

Instructions

1. Type or print this request.
2. Complete *all* items.
3. You are encouraged to discuss this request with your supervisor, but it is not a requirement.
4. Résumés or other background information may be attached if desired.
5. Submit your application to the Personnel Department.

Job   Job   Requesting Supervisor's
Title _____ Grade _____ Name_____

Reason I want job listed_____

Does your supervisor   Supervisor's   Telephone
know of this request?   Yes ☐   No ☐   Name_____ ext. _____

If you have not been on your present   SUPERVISOR'S
job for 6 months (nonexempt) or 1 year (ex-   APPROVAL
empt), you must have your supervisor's approval before submitting your request.   _____

Education

Type of school	Name of school	Dates		Diploma or Degree	Major Subject
		To	From		

Figure 15-2B. Application form for internal advancement (reverse).

Here's What I've Done

Name _____

Current Position

| Job | Job | From | To |
Title_____ Grade _____ (mo./yr.) ____ (mo./yr.)_____

Supervisor _____ Telephone ext._____

Description of work _____

_____

_____

_____

Previous Position

| Job | Job | From | To |
Title_____ Grade _____ (mo./yr.) ____ (mo./yr.)_____

Supervisor _____ Telephone ext._____

Company _____ Organization Name_____

Description of Work_____

_____

_____

_____

Special skills, interests, and hobbies _____

_____

_____

_____

success on the job. This is important, because there are about five losers to every winner.

The personnel department closely monitors the program, posting the job, setting up the interviews, and arranging transfer dates for winning candidates. Openings filled by this program approach 70 percent. And it's not unusual for two or more people to get new jobs as the result of a single opportunity. Freedom to apply and transfer makes this program work.

A second way to find in-house talent is to evaluate people in action. For instance, a selection decision may depend on how capably a person reacts to crisis. Here's an example of what I mean. A bearded, tough-looking, streetwise ruffian challenged petite little Mrs. Smith at her teller's window. He tooked immense as he pushed across a note which read: "This is a stickup. Give me all your money or I'll kill you." Without batting an eye, Mrs. Smith wrote on the note: "Look pretty, big fellow, they're taking your picture." She handed it back and the would-be robber fled. That's keeping cool.

Are your talent scouts alert for creative solutions to difficult problems? Will Mrs. Smith be recognized as a potential candidate for bigger and better things? Does keeping her poise in a tight situation indicate a possible career path to a department that puts a premium on working under pressure?

One East Coast company found no women in plant management ranks. Forewomen, yes; managers, no. It decided to establish a management mobility plan to assist women who were capable of doing factory supervision and management. The new program, which has effectively moved women into management jobs, has helped the company discover a previously untapped source of talent.

When faced with an apparent shortage in talent for its managerial posts, a West Coast firm tried a different approach. Its personnel people recognized that professional, administrative, and clerical personnel were a pipeline chock full of future managers. Most were women. But nearly all supervisors and managers were men. Change was needed. The trick was to discover who to develop and promote. Their program had two steps. Step 1 was to set up a skills bank. To qualify for it, employees were required to list their skills on a special data collection form. (See Figure 15-3A.) The reverse side is an optional career planning form on which the applicant evaluates himself. (See Figure 15-3B.) The completed forms give you a file of volunteers who have talent they want to develop.

Step 2 requires that the supervisor fill out a data form on the applicant. (See Figure 15-4.) The information is reviewed by the personnel office. Departmental and individual strengths, weaknesses, and training requirements are evaluated. Departmental plans are coordinated with staffing requirements as they relate to hiring, promotions, development of training programs, and other efforts. In this way, people who desire advancement are given a chance to match their interests to company requirements, and supervisors get to assess available talent.

What these progressive firms have in common is the desire to keep the supervisor in the selection process. In many companies today, personnel departments have taken over all screening and evaluation. In some cases they decide rates of pay too.

Do you face the situation of the supervisor in a large north central engineering firm who can hire only personnel who have been screened by a recruiter? He cannot give his employees merit increases once they have reached an arbitrary grade maximum. He is required to perform clerical personnel duties, including filling out management development records (never to be used), identifying high-potential employees (never to be promoted), and putting standard 6 percent merit increases (never to be paid) into a computer-generated salary adjustment program.

This supervisor, who in 1960 could use his own discretion in hiring, firing, paying, and appraising subordinates, is now stuck with a poorly designed, inflexible computer system that has developed to score highly on an EEO compliance review. Unfortunately, it does not select, develop, or supervise people.

Everyone recognizes the capabilities of a graduate from MIT or Wharton School of Business, but unfortunately all our hiring

Figure 15-3A. Data collection form (front).

Skills Bank Deposit Slip

Employee _____ Department_____ Date_____

Education (list schools and special interests):

Group Memberships (indicate offices held):

Professional Experience (list main duties and length of performance):

Communication Skills (written and oral):

Military Experience (list ranks and special training):

Patents:

Foreign Languages (indicate fluency):

Awards (cost savings, certificates of merit, other):

Other Talents:

Experience owning your own business:

Figure 15-3B. Data collection form (reverse).

Career Planning Form

Career Interests and Goals   (Include comments that help us relate your background interests and talents to your goals)

1. What are you doing well that you want to continue?

2. What are you doing that you should or must improve?

3. What are you doing that you don't care to do and will never do well? Be honest!

Personal Evaluation   (Evaluate how well you've achieved your objectives)

1. What do you want to accomplish during your working life? (Think in both concrete and abstract terms—for example, money, status, improved family life, improved health.)

2. What do you value most highly? Where do you set your priorities?

3. How have you been doing recently regarding your goals and priorities?

4. Have you challenged yourself enough? Have you capitalized on your strengths, or are you trying to overcome weaknesses?

Figure 15-4. Supervisor's evaluation form.

Skills Bank Supervisor Remarks

Employee_____ Department _____ Date _____

Supervisor_____ Supervised employee From____To____

Experience Evaluation (List employee strengths, weaknesses, and developmental needs. Be specific.)

Potential Career Path (Indicate intermediate positions. Staff or line? Estimate time needed in each.)

Rating of Overall Potential (Support your answer with reasons and examples.)

10	9	8	7	6	5	4	3	2	1

choices aren't that easy. Talent for accounting, engineering, production, and sales jobs often comes in disguise. To maximize your chances of finding it, develop a prospector's approach. Identify what you need. As you develop true prospector's skill, train your colleagues in personnel too. Concentrate on finding the treasure that is available from every individual's potential. Get to the heart of employment priorities. By positively seeking talent, you'll find people available to solve problems and to build a strong and loyal organization. The gold mine you discover will enrich your career too.

16

A Bounty on Wolves

Every department is comprised of employees with different personality traits. One of the supervisor's tasks is to mold them into a cohesive, productive unit. This can be one of the more challenging assignments you will face. It requires that you evaluate your performance as an individual and as part of several groups that exist in your company.

You can separate activities into two broad categories: group efforts and individual efforts. Look at your subordinates and observe patterns in their work performance too. To some extent, these patterns will be defined by the nature of the work objectives. Duties such as paying bills and issuing invoices and deposits can best be done by individuals working alone. But planning new products, designing complex systems, and making capital investment decisions are group-oriented tasks.

The personalities of the people involved in a task play an important role in job success. They shouldn't be overlooked. Personal identity is really a concise collection of habits. The traits you display are the characteristics of your personality. The same goes for your peers and subordinates. Habits can be changed; so can traits. This means people can "change" too. An individual's personality and the situation he faces can *force* him to play certain roles. Let's examine two extremes.

162

PROMOTERS AND LONE WOLVES

Work assignments in a typical environment aren't always fully covered by standard operating procedures. Most duties are open to some degree of personal interpretation. This identification of activities and resources necessary to achieve objectives requires personal choice.

The "promoter" is at one end. His routine response to assignments is to draw on the ideas, advice, and cooperation of everyone who can help complete the effort. He is a habitual meeting caller. He relies on others to contribute all the elements of a solution, then commits himself to the consensus. In many settings this approach quickly solves the problem and completes the assignment. Everyone spots the promoter. He is routinely promoted.

At the other extreme is the "lone wolf." He prefers to do it all himself. He is apprehensive about group involvement. He will research policy manuals, documents, related situations, reference books, and other sources. He develops solutions by deductive reasoning and achieves objectives with a minimum of help from others. Being a lone wolf is not bad. Because his typical response to a problem is to rely on his personal resources, the lone wolf is especially suited for such "back room" functions as research, analysis, and auditing.

Many organizations today look only at the group-oriented personality in identifying management potential. The promoter with ambition is a good bet to make it to top management. But you can't afford to overlook or disqualify quiet, apparently withdrawn people in your group. Lone wolves like Henry David Thoreau, Albert Einstein, and Greta Garbo have made significant contributions to society. But as a supervisor in an organization, would you find it hard to visualize how you might use any of these three brilliant people in your department?

Because of their intelligence, education, and initiative, lone wolves may leave the group behind, performing better as individuals. This may make you uncomfortable. But you may improve your results by coordinating your knowledge, experience, and skills with that of lone wolf subordinates and peers.

As a supervisor, you should recognize the individual characteristics of subordinates and relate job assignments and personnel development activities to them. Unless the lone wolf's boss works with him to focus on progress toward mutual objectives, his capabilities will probably be underutilized. This special attention is necessary because the lone wolf is not likely to take the initiative. He may be content to do only what is asked of him, seeking help only when absolutely necessary. The rest of the time he keeps his nose clean and stays out of "trouble." But if someone else is given credit for his ideas, his resentment may cause further withdrawal and less commitment to his work. Worse still, he may feel that he isn't getting a fair deal. Result: One less supporter for you.

Make sure you do not lose contributions by overlooking the lone wolf. The key is to find ways to utilize the positive aspects of the lone wolf's personality. Think of the functions performed by your department. As we have seen, not every job calls for group involvement. People who work best alone should be given assignments that capitalize on this trait. Matching employees to the right job can be as critical to an organization's success as matching customers to the right products. Recognize that there are distinct benefits to having some lone wolves around. For example, lone wolves:

Avoid cliques.
Are stable employees (don't job-hop).
Concentrate on job duties.
Provide an untapped reservoir of ideas.
Work with little supervision.
Are highly responsive to recognition.
Are dependable performers.
Have an independent attitude.
Rarely engage in "politics."
Cost less (don't compare salaries).

Next, think of the personalities of the people working in your department. Are there some who prefer to work alone? Are the lone wolf people doing the lone wolf jobs? To analyze this question in depth, you should find out how much time your employees spend in group interactions. You can do this by having each subordinate jot down what he's doing at 15-minute intervals—and who he's doing it with. Another approach is to give the same or similar assignments to two or three different people and compare their responses. Or you can conduct a personal time analysis by strolling through your department at various intervals. Note the work flow and working (social) relationships. Social and work activities are sometimes difficult to distinguish. If two people who have no work in common are talking, "join the conversation" to find out their purpose.

You can summarize your findings on a simple chart like that in Figure 16-1. In this example, Ann is a lone wolf and Jack is a promoter. Neither may be performing up to potential. Your analysis may help to explain *why* they are apparently having problems. A reassignment of duties may help them both become more productive.

It is possible, too, that social pressures in the work environment are inhibiting group participation. In-groups and favoritism can be demotivating forces breeding the antisupervisory, antigroup feelings of *lobo* wolf behavior. The absence of feedback and other personal attention from the supervisor can also dampen employee morale. An organization with these destructive influences can bring on the big, bad lobo wolf symptoms even in promoter-type employees. So, before you neatly and negatively categorize a subordinate as a lobo wolf—someone who stays outside the pack, having destructive tendencies— you'd be wise to analyze whether this is really his nature or just a withdrawal from what he perceives to be a hostile environment.

Also recognize that some people are just bashful, hesitant to join into group activities. With patience these people can be trained to overcome their shyness. As you work with them, you will also learn how competent they are and improve their confidence. Regular personal contact, if conducted in an atmosphere free of fear, will often bring these wallflowers into the pack. As a by-product, you may also uncover employees who are attempting to avoid detection.

If a lone wolf expresses aspirations to become a supervisor, he will need to develop skills in group interaction. Indeed, a supervisor needs a blend of the qualities of the lone wolf and the promoter. Individual strengths must be complemented by the ability to organize and participate in group efforts.

Figure 16-1. Time observations.

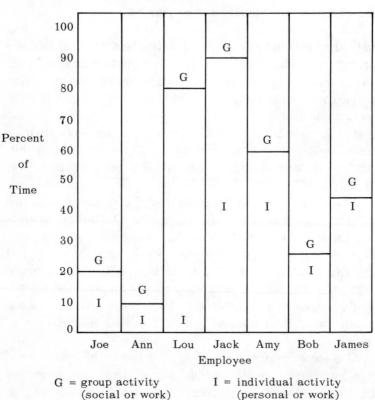

G = group activity   I = individual activity
 (social or work)   (personal or work)

Remember that an integral part of a supervisor's job is achieving objectives through the efforts of subordinates. However, this does not mean the candidate must transform his personality to that of a promoter. He can stay independent. One approach is to put your lone wolf into a group of other lone wolves. There he can practice supervisory techniques without being exposed to severe "promoter" competition. As he becomes more confident in his ability to work with others, you can try him in more aggressive groups.

You should also recognize that some individuals can be highly effective in both roles. Charles Lindbergh demonstrated that he could perform successfully in both individual and group efforts. He worked with others in opening new South American air routes and in developing a mechanical heart. Yet he is best remembered for his individual achievement of making the first solo flight across the Atlantic Ocean. Because of this feat the public quickly dubbed him "The Lone Eagle."

It has been noted that all people are self-made: the successes and the failures. The failures just don't take credit for it. The lone wolf is not always ready to accept sole responsibility for his position in life, but his natural inclination is to look within himself for strengths upon which to build.

To develop career plans for the lone wolf, then, you must stress either the upgrading of technical abilities or the addition of group-oriented skills. It's your job to identify these people and help them choose between a technical career or one in management. It is well worth your efforts. Your reward for trying may be to launch some high-flying Lone Eagles—and one of them could be you.

PART IV

Remember to Supervise Yourself

17

Find Your Real Boss

Supervisor A says to Supervisor B, "If you see my boss, point him out to me." Did you ever hear (or say) that?

Have you ever wished you were your own boss? You can be, right where you are. Right now. I'm not suggesting "moonlighting." To be your own boss you don't have to own and operate a business. You can be your own boss while you are employed and paid by someone else. Don't misunderstand. To determine if you are your own boss, the question is not "Where is your box on the company's organization chart?" In most firms you can easily find that out. Figure 17-1 depicts a "normal" organization with a multilevel hierarchy. You will fit into one of the seven levels. But whether you are in Level 1 (the bottom) or Level 7 (chief executive officer), the challenge in the title is the same.

As supervisor it is especially important for you to be able to answer the question, "Who's your boss?" It may not be who you think it is. I submit that you are your boss. You work for yourself. It's a fact! And those supervisors who recognize it are a lot better off than others. I agree that it may not always seem like you're the boss. Why not? Because in every job you "take orders" from someone. And on some jobs you get simultaneous, conflicting orders from several people.

Figure 17-1. Classic management hierarchy.

ACCEPTING WORK DIRECTION

Let's see how that works. What I'm going to do is change the question to "Who do you accept work from?" This question has a complicated answer. (See Figure 17-2.) If you're like most people, you take on-the-job work direction from formal and informal sources. The formal sources are part of your on-the-job work environment. They may be solid or dotted line. The solid line indicates a direct reporting relationship (as with your functional manager). The dotted line indicates an indirect, but potentially as strong, reporting relationship (for example, when your job assignments require you to take direction from other managers).

The informal sources (connected with wavy lines, since there are no reporting relationships) are never seen on an organization chart. But they exist and exert powerful influences. These include your spouse, peers, friends, social organizations, and big customers. Some of these influences are so strong that they can have a decisive effect on whether you will even accept a work assignment.

On your job how many of these pseudo-bosses do you work for? If you confidently answered "none," don't be so sure. For any single work assignment you may consciously recognize direction from your superior. However, you are also being influenced subconsciously by informal forces. For instance, how do you react to:

Figure 17-2. The many sources of work direction.

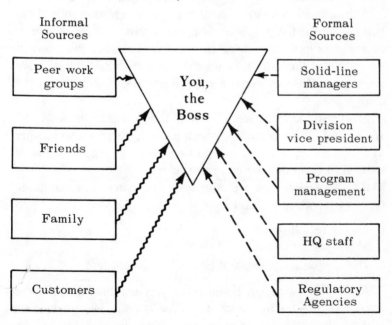

- A neighbor who wants to "visit" for a minute?
- A call from a customer who wants something *now?* (What will you do with the job you are working on?)
- An emergency call from home?
- A friend who says, "Slow down, you're going too fast"?

Many times during your workday you are asked to do two (or more) things at once. Usually setting a priority is simple. If you are your boss, you decide. You smoothly start the most important task while the second waits its turn. No big problem. If you're not the boss, you will lose time (and win a reputation for being indecisive) if you try to get a priority from someone else. Thus two big problems. Now what if the assignments come from *two* top executives? In this case, conflict is possible and the decision gets tougher. Problems can occur unless communications are *open and clear*. To be your own boss, you must be able to decide the priority then communicate it.

Although all communications tools are important, one thing besides the pen is mightier than the sword. What really gets things accomplished is direct face-to-face dialogue. But many of us will delay this talk, thus wasting our most vital and effective asset: time. We may even be wasting our time with top management.

The reason is often fear. We're afraid to make a mistake. So we're afraid to decide and communicate. If you want to prosper as a supervisor, you will have to save yourself. And you'll have to do it in several different organizational formats.

In your career you will probably encounter three common types of reporting relationships:

Solid-line/solid-line
Solid-line/dotted-line
The program management (special team) concept

As you can see from Figure 17-3, any combination of these can cause conflicting directions to be issued. This discussion will be covered in more detail later when we look at the program management relationship.

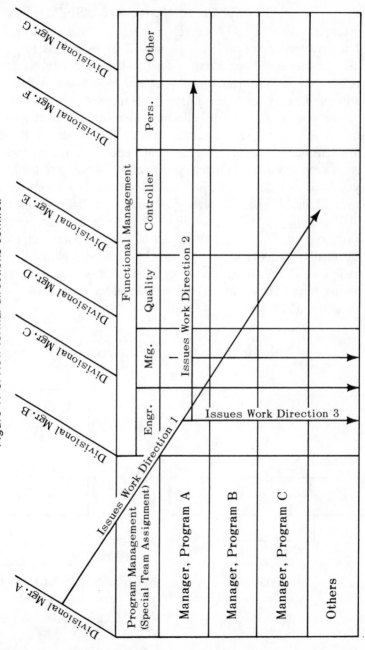

Figure 17-3. How formal directions conflict.

SOLID-LINE/SOLID-LINE RELATIONSHIPS

Accepting work direction involves both risk and opportunity. Early recognition of each is important. Every work task has specific problems and opportunities for building successful working relationships. You should know where you stand with your superiors, peers, and subordinates at all times.

Are you in a solid-line/solid-line organization? In this relationship, you may report directly to one or more people. If they are reasonable, compatible, and uncompetitive, you're lucky. Also keep in mind that unless you're at the very top of the heap you have an indirect solid line to your supervisor's superior too. (See Figure 17-4.) Each can give you work. This produces a visible and an invisible solid line. The visible solid line is in a situation where you directly report to two superiors. This occasionally occurs in service groups. More likely you find the invisible solid line: While you report to your boss, you also report to his boss. They can each give you direct orders—and you must respond.

Figure 17-4. Solid-line work direction.

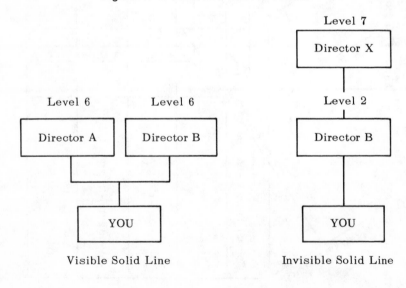

Have you ever taken the tact test? Two seniors direct you in two competing work efforts. Your problem: Choose and lose. In a conflict situation like this you can minimize risk by communicating. You must get the interested parties together. Tell them your problems. *Recommend a solution.* Ask them to approve priority.

If you are really "on the ball" you will make the decision yourself and then call the parties together to explain your solution. If you are right, you gain the respect of your superiors. If you are wrong, you gain additional information (some that may be vital to correctly completing the assignment).

This solution can be illustrated by a sporting event: A poor golfer kept trying to hit the ball. He hit an anthill with every swing. After he did it several times, one of the smarter ants said, "If we want to be saved we had better get on the ball." Get on the ball! Make priority decisions. Practice on minor problems. Turn the problems into opportunities to develop decision-making skills.

React to the situation and the individual. The directions you get from a Level 7 superior must be handled differently from those from a Level 6 superior. However, both may create conflict situations. The key is knowing how to work with people you report to.

In fact, just keeping your manager's next higher echelon informed of progress can be a problem. Not keeping company management up to date on outstanding or weak performances also causes difficulties. You're the boss. You must decide how to solve the problem. It's easier to do that if you concentrate on learning how people think.

A lot of information, procedures, and techniques are available to solve these problems. Almost every college and university has special management classes that deal with the most difficult of these problems. You can learn more about people by studying transactional analysis (TA). You can improve your social and language skills to control and dissipate management tensions.

What prevents you from starting the task? What motivates you and others in your firm to put up with directional problems? Could it be apathy? Think about it. Your apathy may be creating unnecessary on-the-job tensions in yourself and others. You can learn to release these tensions and develop new on-the-job skills.

There is no law that says subordinates cannot profit from their supervisor at the same time that the supervisor is profiting from them. This kind of "everybody wins" environment is easier to achieve in an atmosphere of frankness. It is not the sole responsibility of the senior person to create this atmosphere; the junior can and must help.

When you take an assignment from any "boss," talk it over until you are confident you understand it. As the work progresses, notify the boss of conflicts or problems. When you present a problem, be sure you have some recommendations ready for dealing with it.

When you report on operations to your solid-line seniors, make sure the data you generate really fills the order. If you have any doubts, talk them over with your "boss." Then deliver them to the senior. Also, don't assume that the facts your supervisor ordered are identical to what "Director B" wants. Report to the person, not the position. Why? Because people's requirements vary widely, depending on their education, experience, level in the organization, aptitudes, concern for detail, and other factors.

SOLID-LINE/DOTTED-LINE RELATIONSHIPS

One ad for a seminar on communication skills proclaims:

> Do you see yourself in this ad? *Wanted:* A special person to help a *busy* executive. Must be responsible, self-motivated, and willing to grow. Excellent human relations and administrative skills required. This position involves working closely and effectively with other people. The successful applicant will be able to solve and/or prevent problems in communication and understanding.

These skills are particularly needed in a formal solid-line/dotted-line reporting relationship. In Figure 17-5, Managers B, C, D, and E report directly to A. However, C, D, and E also are required to do work for B. This relationship arises when it becomes necessary to receive orders from or give them to someone who doesn't report to you. Such orders do not, of course, have the force of those received from solid-line managers. (For example, an instruction from the controller to the personnel manager.)

The dotted-line relationship requires you to have an impact on someone else. If your manager expects you to have such an impact, you must have some power beyond your personal influence to get the assignment accepted and completed. This is particularly true if you are in a staff department, where your skills must play a part in the decisions of others.

The dotted-line/solid-line relationship can be a difficult one to

Figure 17-5. Solid-line and dotted-line relationships.

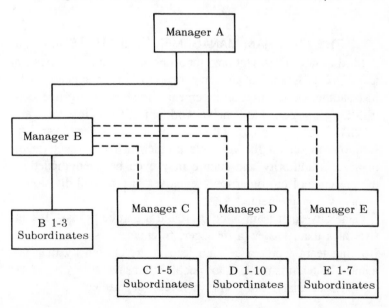

work with. It may introduce conflicting directions into work assignments and lead to lowered morale, loyalty questions (personal versus organizational), and duplication of effort. In addition, questions can arise on who gets reported to first. Data may be restricted from some groups or used against others. Confusion may also arise in the mind of the dotted-line manager who believes he has solid-line authority, or through the conflicts that result from different instructions in different locations or workers who have different beliefs.

This organizational environment can be created by the simultaneous activities of a staff manager (controller or personnel) on the one hand and a functional head (divisional vice president) on the other. A functional head may feel affronted and deprived of authority if a staffer seemingly interfaces with his or her operation. The staff manager may react in a similar way when directed by the functional head.

The two-boss problem arouses tensions. The "social" scene becomes more complex. Again, clear and open communication can help solve the problem.

THE PROGRAM MANAGEMENT RELATIONSHIP

A third type of organizational reporting structure is the "special team" or program management relationship. It appears to be just another dotted-line arrangement. However, solid-line controls are also needed to achieve work objectives. Timeliness and efficiency are the goals. Often a special work team can find solutions to seemingly insoluble problems. The project (team) manager's authority and stature may even be strengthened by the presence of customer representatives or top-level division or company management.

Generally each team is built around a particular task. It consists of a team leader (a manager, foreman, or supervisor) and working team members. Team leaders are chosen by management. The team is made up of people from several levels (supervisors, specialists, and peers) in several departments.

Under this arrangement, the leader may be managing an operation that cuts horizontally across vertical lines. This is probably the toughest problem facing task forces. Expert interpersonal communications are required to make the system work. Of the three kinds of reporting arrangements, this is the most demanding one for a supervisor, since it requires difficult decisions about accepting work direction. To complicate matters, your firm may even create several different reporting arrangements at the same time. You can simultaneously be supervising different, even competing, organizational structures (formal and informal).

BE YOUR OWN BOSS

Still, you are your own boss. You can rise in your organization if you:

Communicate efficiently and logically.
Learn when and how to get help.
Decide priorities.
Take some risks.

You don't have to be an independent businessman to be your own boss. But you do have to be able to recognize organizational differences and personal needs of others. Most importantly, you must learn to evaluate your situation, react to it, and effectively direct yourself to accomplishing your goals.

Why wait for someone else to tell you what to do? Give yourself an order. After all, you're the boss.

18

A Budget Is Your Plan

The morning mail brings a letter from the president. "Greetings," it begins. No, you aren't being drafted into the Army. Something worse is in store for you. This letter is from your firm's president. It seems his idea of basic training is to get you to develop a meaningful budget. The usual objective of a budget is to set a goal, measure progress, evaluate that progress, and decide. This seems very straightforward. Yet usually only the controller, the budget director, or someone with the title of industrial engineer really seems to care about developing skills in budgeting. Supervisors in engineering, personnel, sales, and production frown when they hear the term "budget." They would like someone else to creatively design a profit into every month, product, operation, process, and program. Unfortunately, a few time study experts or accountants can't do the job alone. They need a lot of help to measure and control costs. Yes, most firms are still in business to design, develop, manufacture, and sell profitable products and provide profitable services. Even nonprofit organizations ultimately expect to match income to costs. Government units also spend considerable time developing revenue and expense projections.

LEARNING HOW TO BUDGET

Learning how to budget expenses (deciding which ones to incur) is a management development task that must be performed effectively if the firm is to succeed. Yet many supervisors pay little attention to planning and controlling costs—and very quickly get into trouble. The smart supervisor soon learns that becoming expert in budgeting is a profitable use of time. Properly done, it gives him a chance to think like his boss, the general manager, or the president of his firm. It forces the supervisor to relate what he wants to do to what the firm can afford. More about this later.

Effective budgeting is the act of putting a dollar price tag on your operating plans, then selling them. Your budget tells management what you expect to spend in some future period. As such, it serves as one more channel of communication.

On first glance, budgeting seems simple enough. Just plan the next period like the current one. Costs appear to be controllable in total. Unless your company or department is new, historical data are readily available from accounting records. Spending rates can apparently be set on the basis of:

Previous experience (1, 3, 12 months, or longer).
Annualizing the current year, using:
   A workday factor
   A machine usage factor
   A weekly factor
   An average monthly spending rate
   Operation standards

Unfortunately, this is not the way the future will happen. And therein lies the problem. Few historical costs directly relate to a single product, project, job, or future time period. Instead, plans for the future relate to what your company "can afford," which in turn is affected by changes in laws, salesmen's performance, production efficiency, new machines, computers, and hundreds of other unknown (and thus uncontrollable) variables.

As a result, trying to tell you how to budget your operation is like the situation my sister ran into in India. She hired an electrician to do some work in her apartment. The man kept coming to her for instructions concerning how to do this and that. Finally, exasperated, she said, "You know what has to be done. Why not just go ahead and use your common sense?"

"Madam," said the young Indian with becoming gravity, "common sense is a gift of God. All I have is a technical education."

It takes more than a technical education to create a budget that will work for you. It takes judgment too. Stringent financial cost control is difficult. There are many dangers to using the past to predict the future. Trends are not precise predictors of significant changes in direction. Some costs can't be annualized. A prior year may be unique; an unusually large order or high new product startup costs may require changes in resource allocation. Different size orders, abandonment of old products or plants, new regulations, losing a key person, noncompetitive salaries, opening a new plant, or a dry spell of no orders can instantly wreck a beautifully conceived and supported budget.

Despite these apparent problems, most supervisors are required to develop a set of plans, stated in financial terms. You already do this planning in one fashion or another. Through your day-to-day actions and trade-off decisions, you are spending your department's time and resources. In the near term, every action you take has the potential to increase or reduce profit.

To begin the budgeting process all you have to do is formalize your decisions. Prepare a list of decisions and, for each one, estimate the resources required and their cost. The next step is to justify your decisions (budget) to your boss. In the process, you will do more than "sell" the boss; you will also increase your commitment to achieve your plans. And the justification doesn't have to generate a mountain of paperwork. An effective way to support a budget (with management and other auditors) is to provide a written rationale. In most budget systems, the computer summarizes numbers. (See Figure 18-1.) Generally, narrative support for budget items is also needed.

Figure 18-1. Departmental budget recap.

```
                                    DATE:      01/01/79
                                    PERIOD:    04/01/79 - 03/31/80



                                             BASE
                               ESTIMATED     LABOR            TOTAL
DIRECT LABOR                     HOURS       RATE/HR.        DOLLARS

ACCTG. CODE       LABOR CATEGORY

  0001            Assembly        12,480     $13.38      $   166,980
  0002            Fabrication     34,760       8.29          288,158.
  0004            Inspection      15,260       4.25           64,855

                  Sub Total Non Professional Labor       $   519,993

  0011            Design Engineers  4,160    $11.16      $    46,426
  0012            Technicians     57,240       8.62          493,411
  0015            Drafting        12,388       4.60           56,985

                  Sub Total Professional Labor           $   596,822

         Total Labor            136,288                   $1,116,815

Overseas Allowances:  None
Non Professional Escal Rate (9.0% of $519,993)   $46,802
Professional Escal Rate (7.4% of $596,822)        44,164
         Total Escal                                          90,966
Labor Overhead (14.0% of $566,795)                79,350
Labor Overhead (14.0% of $640,986)                89,738
         Total Overhead                                      169,088
         Total Direct Labor                              $1,376,869
                               Base              Material
Material                       Dollars  Overhead %  Overhead

Purchased                    $ 12,814    10%     $ 1,281
Sub-Contract>$1 million        25,966     1%         260
Major Sub-Contract < 1M        71,915     1%         719
         Total Material      $110,695            $ 2,260   $   112,955


Other Direct Costs:

Trips 339 @ various rates                         85,675
Per Diem: 1,097 days @ $46 per day                50,462
Auto 1,083 days @ $23 per day                     24,909
Other miscellaneous costs                         56,456
         Total Other Direct Costs                            217,502
         Total Cost                                       $1,707,326

Profit/Fee on costs @ 10%                                    170,733
Revenue required to cover department
costs incurred and return a normal profit                $1,878,059

     Note: 1)Escalation rate is the average salary increase
             percentage caused by planned merit, cost of
             living or promotional increases.
           2)Some values will vary slightly due to rounding caused by
             average rates.
```

Costs fall into four general categories (your situation may require more or less):

Labor costs
Labor-related costs
Materials and supplies
Other direct costs

Each of these is illustrated with several examples in the Appendix to this chapter.

It's very difficult for an enlightened management to argue with specific, identified spending plans. By being specific, you move yourself a step (and a few dollars) ahead of the supervisor who can muster only generalities. In generating specific plans, you can also avoid a lot of the games that can be played on unwary supervisors. Supervisors and executives experienced in manipulating numbers for their own benefit have several tricks up their sleeves. To protect yourself and your department, you should be aware of these so you can point them out and get them stopped.

DEFENSIVE BUDGETING

Learn to budget defensively. We all look to "management" for top-down direction. The budget cycle is a prime example. Some managements will issue overall guidelines. After these are met and apparently approved, someone up there changes his mind. New directions are issued.

One ploy that often confuses supervisors is the "stretch" plan. A stretch plan is one that requires a commitment to exceed originally planned performance. This can be accomplished in several ways. One is for management to demand a 10 percent cut in costs (across the board) with no reduction in service or output and no exceptions. A second is to ask certain organizational elements to sign up for higher sales targets (or greater output), while incurring costs at the originally planned level. A third is to make specific reductions to selected accounts. For instance, training might be eliminated, advertising cut back, travel reduced, or maintenance deferred.

In effect, a stretch plan is a renegotiation of an earlier agreement. Don't be confused by this management gimmick. When it occurs, be sure you can document exceptions. You can sometimes gain exemption. There's not much you can do about a stretch plan, but some scarred veterans of the budget wars try. They pad their budgets and argue effectively enough to carry an extra 15 or 20 percent right through the original approval cycle. They know from past experience that the first submission won't be the last. (One Midwestern company ran 34 budget iterations in one year.)

Generally speaking, management expects costs to follow income or volume. If income is expected to go up 10 percent, management will issue a top-down guideline directing that costs grow less than 10 percent. Thus profit is sure to grow. This feeling persists despite inflation rates in double figures.

Fixed and Variable Costs

But be wary. By their very nature, cost growth targets produce surprises. Bear in mind that some costs are variable and may be directly controllable by you; others are not. Some are fixed for a certain range of operations. Others vary directly with staffing, sales, or any number of variables. Identify them and their impact on your organization. Here is a list that may help:

VARIABLE ACCOUNTS
    Administration
    Advertising
    Clerical
    Donations
    Electricity
    Engineers
    Expensed equipment
    Freight
    Fuel

Janitors
Manufacturing materials
Meetings and meals
Operating supplies
Overtime premium
Postage
Printing
Shift bonus
Travel
FIXED ACCOUNTS
Amortization
Depreciation
General taxes and insurance
Marketing
Rentals
Supervision
Telephone

Some variable expenses aren't as controllable as they seem. A prime example is the group of labor-related costs known as "fringe benefits," which include federal, state, and local payroll taxes (including FICA), employee group insurance, pension and annuity plans, holidays, vacation, and worker's compensation. The costs of these items directly relate to people—and so appear to be easily controllable. However, their rate is dependent on company policies and the directives of many state and federal bodies.

One Eastern manufacturer issued its overall cost growth guidelines at 6 percent. This seemed reasonable to everyone until six months later a 9 percent growth in fringe costs was received. Over 30 percent of the costs to be incurred were fringe costs. This meant that other costs could increase only about 4 percent. Rebudgeting was required, at considerable expense.

An important aspect of defensive budgeting is to minimize the number of "fixed" accounts in your department. Fixed costs aren't controllable. They occur whether you get a great deal of business or none. Control of fixed costs requires knowledge of the expansion and contraction of your department.

Many costs occur as a *step function*. Let's see how that works. For a short time period, over a given volume, a number of variable costs can be treated as fixed. Supervision is one of these. Assume you can routinely supervise from 2 to 8 people. However, if the number of subordinates in your department grows to 9, 10, or 12, you may start to lose control. As a result, the department is split and a second supervisor is added. A step from one to two supervisors takes place at 8 subordinates. Now two supervisors are a fixed cost until a third is needed. Salesmen and sales territories work much the same way.

A new product line requires capital investment, fixed and variable startup costs, and implied costs of capital to fund an inventory. For a specific planning period, these too may occur as a step function.

Costs usually thought of as being fixed include depreciation, rent, and obsolescence. These change only as assets are added or replaced, facilities are changed, or leases are renegotiated. You are limited in your ability to control them. Note, however, that a step function may exist through overall expansion and contraction of the firm. Once an asset is acquired or a lease signed, the resultant cost is "fixed" for some specific period of time—no matter what the volume of work.

Direct and Indirect Costs

An additional point to keep in mind when budgeting defensively is that costs can be either direct or indirect. Direct costs include production labor, materials, and travel costs that directly benefit a job, project, or product. Indirect costs (sometimes called overhead or burden costs) have no direct benefits. They include dollars spent for administration, paying bills, plant maintenance programs, snow shoveling, general supplies, paper and pencils, and purchasing of sales-related costs. Indirect costs can approach 50 percent of the total cost of your firm's products.

Budgeting indirect costs is a major supervisory problem, because the dollars spent are not directly tied to output. Instead, they are generally "allocated" or distributed to production departments according to an arbitrary allocation rate. The rate is calculated by relating a group of indirect costs to some base, such as square feet of floor space, number of people, total salaries paid, number of telephones, or total nonunion salaries. Ask your company's accountant what formula he uses to make allocations. Once you understand the allocation base, you may be able to reduce the number of costs distributed to you.

The assumption behind allocations is that costs can be collected and redistributed to a specific process, operation, or department. Facility (building space occupance) costs are an example. All expenses incurred for property taxes and insurance, rent, heat, light, power, maintenance, cleanup, and related labor are collected. The square footage of the plant or building is calculated. Simple division of costs by square feet defines an allocation rate of cost per square foot. This rate is used to charge out or distribute all facility costs to individual departments on the basis of square feet occupied. (Vacant space costs you just as much per square foot as productively occupied space.)

You may not feel responsible for occupancy costs because you see space only as a ratio of some other cost—one that is supposed to be controlled by someone else. You're partly right. But you control your space. And keep in mind that if increasing volume forces a second and third shift, with no change in space, the actual cost per square foot can decrease. It's a cheaper way to "add" space then opening a new building.

BUDGET CONTROLS

In some companies, both large and small, controls are completely lacking. Expenses aren't budgeted by or for anyone; they just happen. These include idle or vacant plant and equipment, property taxes on vacant land (whether leased or owned), standby equipment, and obsolete equipment or material. Yet you can be sure that the accountants are distributing these costs to you in one way or another. In fact, these costs pose a double-edged problem. Unused facilities and electronic equipment incur taxes, require investment, maintenance, heat, light, power, calibration, and involve the inventory control system. You can reduce your share of these costs by getting rid of the items you don't need.

A final word of warning. If supervisors can't control costs, overhead controls may be imposed on them. One Midwestern firm experimented with a concept involving "executives-at-large." This attempt at control required that each vice president be measured on his ability to control a "pool" of expenses incurred outside his normal jurisdiction. For example, the production manager reviewed and jointly authorized costs of running the personnel department. He approved new programs, got involved in union negotiations, and analyzed changes in the fringe benefit program. The chief engineer became involved in the marketing area. He was required to evaluate and approve justifications for an increased sales force. The program worked pretty well and, as a side benefit, demands for service were curtailed. Also, the executives-at-large became more knowledgeable about staff functions. This improved cost awareness caused a few arguments, but the resolution was constructive. And staff supervisors reported that the give-and-take, cost savings, and visibility to management were worth their efforts.

As a supervisor interested in budgeting and cost control, you must demand greater visibility of expenses. Account numbers are cheap, but many accounting departments refuse to issue more than a bare minimum. The result is that control of overhead tends to be lumped in one account. Mismanagement can result. Overhead costs become invisible via the allocation process.

Here is an example of how overhead costs can "get lost." A Western company originally used a single supplies account. Its management noticed that spending for supplies fluctuated wildly from month to month. Management challenged supervisors to control this problem area. They complained that they couldn't. A detailed review revealed that the expenses incurred could be segregated into eight related but different cost classifications: operating supplies, stores supplies, expensed tools, expensed office equipment, office supplies, preprinted forms, reproduction/copy costs, and fixture supplies. Five of these accounts caused the wild gyrations; three were relatively stable. Result: Eight new subaccounts were established. Each was assigned to one individual who was given responsibility for controlling spending. Individual account budgets were prepared for management review and approval. This involved obtaining input from user organizations and setting up a charge-out system. Costs were reported against the approved plans and distributed directly to the benefiting organizations. Today, deviations from plan are minimal, and the "swingers" are under control. Charges to benefiting departments are visible.

Because of all the variations in cost distribution systems, budgets sometime cause confusion and raise problems in setting priorities. Three factors are involved. First, many managements have not taken the time to establish supervisory measurement criteria. Budgeting and reporting are left to the supervisor's discretion. Management doesn't measure results. Thus controlling costs becomes a no-win situation. To avoid this problem, you must insist on recognition of achievement for meeting budget commitments. Demand that credit or blame be attached to meeting, beating, or missing budget targets. Make sure these questions are answered: "How much spending is enough?" "Who is responsible?" "Are the right things getting done?"

Second, different and often conflicting points of view come into play in the budgeting process. The person performing "service" for you can always defend more spending. He wants to give you better service. And if you don't have to pay the full cost, you may help him spend more by demanding more. Thus the service provider feels he can't spend enough. At the same time, management may feel (but be unable to prove) that he is spending too much.

The third factor involves productivity. The so-called service functions are slow to create new productive methods. They aren't specifically required to earn a profit. While creative engineers and factory personnel strive to reduce costs, develop improved techniques, and invent new products, the same drive is generally *not* expected from service functions. Insist that cost reduction goals be assigned to the service departments.

Defensive supervisory budget control can help your firm make money. How? Estimate the cost for each product. Budget, fact-find, analyze, and get approval for each element. Let's run through a quick analysis to see how this works.

Assume your company has an apparent total overhead budget of $100,000. The base for distribution is total salaries paid, which is planned at $500,000. The resultant overhead application rate will be 20 percent ($100,000 ÷ $500,000). All production work is quoted using the 20 percent rate. This means that every dollar of direct labor will absorb 20¢ of overhead. However, many customers ask for quotes. As a result, bids are prepared and submitted totalling $800,000 in labor. Does that mean $160,000 (800,000 × .20) in overhead will be needed? No—for two reasons. First, there are some fixed costs in the $100,000. Second, not all bids will result in orders. If orders with labor requirements of only $600,000 are actually won by your firm, what will the overhead spending be? Should the budget control value be $120,000?

If the overhead rate is completely variable, the overhead recovered and spent will be $120,000 (.20 × $600,000). But the overhead is not 100 percent variable. It may be all fixed (at $100,000), as planned. Will the extra $20,000 ($120,000 − $100,000) be spent, or will some or all of it become extra profit to your firm? It takes detailed analysis to find the answers.

What if overhead budgets aren't all spent? If the actual rate should turn out to be 18 percent, at $500,000 in labor, overhead spending should be only $90,000 (.18 × $500,000). Does your budgeting system routinely identify the variance early enough to benefit you and your firm? Will an underrun automatically lead to lower prices? Will it increase profit? Or will $100,000 be spent? Considerable financial analysis is required to determine the "best" answer for your firm. You can be in the forefront of the analysis of your department.

GET FULL VALUE FOR YOUR MONEY

When you decide to spend money, be sure you get full value for it. As you do your job, ask yourself and your subordinates these questions:

Is it in the budget?
Is this work required?
Could the work be eliminated?
Do I really need this item now?
Can I stay on schedule by doing this work?
Am I charging the right account?
Does this need to be the "best" product in the world? (Remember, best is in the eyes of the beholder. Your best may not be what your customer wants.)

As you answer these questions, your ability to budget and control costs will improve. You will increase your chances of making a profit—and of growing into a job with larger, more complex budgets. Do your homework. Practice. Perfect your skill in defensive budgeting today. It's one less lesson to learn tomorrow.

APPENDIX
A BUDGET RATIONALE

Labor Costs
Manpower

Each individual in the Program Financial Control organization is responsible for financial support on customer contracts to help meet our profit goals. They must assure the costs are accurate and concur with the company financial policy and objectives. They must also ensure the validity of the CSTAR cost system and issue reports in a timely manner. The functions and areas of responsibility for each person in the Program Financial Control department are summarized below.

MANPOWER SUMMARY (Subaccount 201)

Position Description	Grade	Hours
Supervisor (1)	8	2,080
Cost analyst (1)	5	2,080
Cost analyst, associate (2)	2	4,160
Cost analyst, associate (1)	2	2,080
		10,400

MANPOWER SUMMARY (Subaccount 300)

Position Description	Grade	Hours
Cost analyst, assistant	14	2,080
Total (Subaccounts 201 and 300)		12,480

J. L. Hogan, Supervisor—Class 0201
Responsible for directing, planning, and delegating all Program Financial Control activity, financial support for contracts and program management, and coordination of the profit plan, associated areas, and year-end audit and purge activity. The purpose of this position is to ensure that divisional financial policies are implemented and followed and that profit goals can be met.

E. Tomas, Cost Analyst—Class 0201
Responsible for providing financial support on the new XYZ product program, bids and proposals, IR&D, and SRA, as well as supporting auditors, closing cost programs, prenegotiation strategy, and providing the Program Budget Expended Report.

R. Jones, Cost Analyst Associate—Class 0201
Responsible for providing financial support on Compass Ears program and TD-1220, and ensuring that CSTAR is accurate on these programs, as well as supporting auditors, prenegotiation strategy, and cost of sales and profit planning.

G. Smith, Cost Analyst Associate—Class 0201
Responsible for providing financial support on MDC/SS, PLSS, and
ASD T&M, and ensuring that CSTAR is accurate on PLSS, as well
as supporting auditors and prenegotiation strategy.

W. Pan, Cost Analyst Assistant—Class 300
Responsible for providing financial support on Helmet Sights, MCG
Spares, service contracts, IDR, and Penny Counter, as well as supporting auditors and prenegotiation strategy. In September 1980 he
will be made a Cost Analyst Associate—Class 0201.

Labor-Related Costs
Fringe Benefits   (Subaccount 3300)
All vacation, holiday, and payroll tax benefits are accounted for
under the labor overhead rate of 27 percent.
Training   (Subaccount 3400)
The supervisor should attend at least one course yearly to keep
abreast of changes in the field of government contracts. Scheduled
courses for fiscal 1980 include:

Cost Accounting Standards
Negotiating Government Contracts
Pricing Production Products

While we try to schedule courses in Zone 1, at times, depending on
sponsor and course content, only Zone 2 is available. Therefore, Zone
2 has been used in the estimate.

Travel	1 trip
Per diem	3 days
Auto rental	3 days

Clerical Services   (Subaccount 6702)
Based on fiscal 1979 actual and projected figures, $1,200 will be
required for fiscal 1980. Clerical services are required for peak workload and other mid-month reporting requirements.

Materials and Supplies
Supplies   (Subaccount 5500)
It is estimated that this control office will use $100 in special
office supplies during fiscal 1980. This estimate is based on actual
usage for fiscal 1979.

Books and Subscriptions   (Subaccount 8100)

Although books are most often purchased through the library, cash purchase of text material is sometimes necessary. Based on fiscal 1979 experience, it is estimated that $42 will be spent in fiscal 1980.

Office Equipment   (Subaccount 8110)

It is estimated that two new calculators will be required for this department. One calculator for the organization's secretary ($100) and one replacement calculator for the supervisor of the department ($150). Total: $250.

Other Office Supplies   (Subaccount 5102)

Based on fiscal 1979 figures, including an 8 percent escalation of cost for supply items such as paper, folders, and pens, the projected amount needed for fiscal 1980 is $240.

Other Direct Costs

Telephone   (Subaccount 6601)

Costs of $25 are estimated to cover toll calls incurred to locate key employees while they are on the road.

Meetings, Lunches, and Dinners   (Subaccount 7700)

Based on fiscal 1979 experience, it is estimated that $1,000 will be incurred to cover costs related to various technical discussions, stay involved with other professionals in the community, and recognize individual achievements.

Travel   (Subaccount 7801)

Estimated travel costs are based on fiscal 1978 and 1979 experience. It is anticipated that the following trips are necessary:

Zone 2	12 trips
Zone 3	1 trip
Per diem	26 days
Auto rental	12 days

The purpose of these trips is to conclude contract negotiations. Schedule furnished upon request.

Postage   (Subaccount 9200)

It is estimated that $100 in postage will be needed to cover after-hours mailing of material to other corporate offices. Experience in fiscal 1979 as modified by our forecast of a 15 percent increase in volume for fiscal 1980 is the basis of this estimate.

19

Can a Supervisor Be
a Part-Time Financial Analyst?

If supervisors want to succeed, they must learn how to use financial tools. Why? Because a sale without a profit is not a sale—it's a donation. A department without cost analysis isn't a department—it's a country club. In some departments "profit" and "cost" may be tough to pin down. Make an effort to do it. The benefits are well worth the effort, because more opportunities for promotion occur in a profitable, growing, cost-conscious company than in an unprofitable one.

Are you designing profits into your reports, systems, or products? Do you regularly use the analytical tools available to determine the most profitable administrative, engineering, production, or sales applications?

COST SAVINGS AND PROFIT RETURN

The assignment of priorities for supervisory activities involves several factors. One of the first considerations is cost savings and profit return. In general, projects (whether product, system, or policy related) with the best profit potential should be worked on first. Projects with little profit potential should be deferred, delayed, or perhaps abandoned altogether.

The financial analyst in your company can help you find cost savings or new profit opportunities. At your firm he may be called the "price analyst," "cost accountant," or "budget analyst." Whatever his label, he has skills that can help. Use him. Ask him to teach you the basic techniques of cost-profit analysis. By applying yourself, you can aim your efforts at those items that build profit.

What can he do for you? First, the financial analyst can show you how easy it is to keep necessary records. You should use these records to routinely analyze significant revenues and costs. We'll use a sales management situation to illustrate some straightforward analytical techniques. These can also be used to evaluate production orders, job tickets, engineering efforts, invoice processing, and other operating costs.

In our mock sales department, we'll start by calculating the average selling cost per call of Joe Smith and see how it relates to his average sales per call. The basic calculations involve the following data:

Number of calls		200
Selling costs		
Salary	$1,000	
Commissions	500	
Transit	2,500	
Total		$ 4,000
Total sales		$62,000

Thus the average cost per call is $20 ($4,000 ÷ 200), and the average sales per call is $310 ($62,000 ÷ 200).

This information is a handy yardstick for measuring individual performance. Now you know that whenever Joe is not writing $15.50 ($310 ÷ $20) in sales orders for every dollar he spends, he is below his average. His accounts can be analyzed to find those worth repeat sales and those to drop.

This may seem like a lot of dull numbers, but the calculations are easy, and an improvement in results could brighten your chances for a bonus. Pick a period and a salesperson to analyze. A month is probably better than a quarter or a year, since close control requires frequent cost-effective monitoring. You decide the frequency you need. Weekly monitoring may cost more than the data are worth.

The next step is to compare Joe's performance with the overall company average. If it is $10 of sales per dollar of sales expense, you know Joe is doing a better than average job. The analyst will want to know how Joe does it: great territory or great techniques. Analyzing Joe's performance may help you find sales techniques that can benefit your entire department.

GROSS MARGIN AND OTHER FACTORS

That was an easy one. Let's make it more complicated. Assume your company has three products: Grade 1, Label 2, and Brand 3. There are several analytical techniques you can use to find out which product to push. Time analysis may disclose that 10 percent of sales time is spent on Brand 3; sales analysis indicates 70 percent of the sales are Brand 3. These data suggest that Brand 3 is the leader and that you should be pushing it.

What may be hidden is that Brand 3 has a poor gross margin: only 5 percent. Gross margin is the difference between product selling price and production costs. For Brand 3, a $500 sale nets only $25. This $25 must cover the direct selling expense plus an allocation of costs for administration, product development, obsolescence, interest, and *profit*. Should you push Brand 3? You can't tell without additional analyses. Related factors to consider include production, lead times, possibility of cost improvements, price-volume relationships, and profit.

Time is a critical factor in the profit picture for any firm. Time is money. The more time spent in decision making, design, production, or sales, the more your company must charge for the product. If the costs can't be passed on, the company will suffer a loss. In today's competitive marketplace higher prices may result in lost sales.

The design of new products, and the reevaluation of existing products, must consider possible changes in the costs of components. New materials must be adopted rapidly throughout the product life cycle as developments are announced. Do you know what they are? Profitability requires quick engineering turnaround. With the wild cost fluctuations of the 1970s many firms had to redesign their products to stay competitive. Cost trade-off studies between components and production techniques did the job.

Inflation is a major problem for every company. However, the inflation factor becomes more critical for products with a long lead time (the time it takes to get the product built and shipped). From the previous example, your analyst may find that typical lead times are:

Product	Lead Time
Grade 1	6 months
Label 2	3 months
Brand 3	1 month

According to this analysis, it takes six times longer for Grade 1 to become revenue than for Brand 3. Thus a new problem quietly enters. With Grade 1's longer lead time, inflationary cost increases may occur. Add fixed sales prices to increasing costs and the result is reduced profits. This suggests that products with a long lead time must be carefully priced. A discount from list price on Brand 3 may aid sales and profits. The same strategy for Grade 1 may mean disaster. Grade 1 sales contracts may even need an escalation clause to guard against this risk.

An analysis of investment costs of Grade 1 will show that they exceed that of Label 2 and Brand 3. Why? Because the product stays in inventory so much longer. This may lead to cash flow problems too. An increase in orders for Grade 1 may require a loan to finance the inventory.

ORDER BACKLOG

These problems are predictable. With the data obtained, an analysis of one more item—order backlog—gives an early warning of trouble. Order backlog is the dollar value of signed sales orders to be shipped (or perhaps to be built). This analysis can help point your efforts in the most profitable directions. By categorizing backlog, your analyst may find:

Product	Backlog Last Year	Backlog This Year
Grade 1	$ 500,000	$ 100,000
Label 2	500,000	500,000
Brand 3	500,000	1,400,000
	$1,500,000	$2,000,000

The total backlog is up a whopping 33 percent ($500,000 ÷ $1,500,000). Sales for the coming year are up for sure. Will it be a profitable one? A gross margin analysis of the backlog is shown in Table 19-1. As the analysis suggests, this company is in for a nasty surprise. Even with backlog up 33 percent, the potential gross margin is down $155,000. The overall gross margin is down from a respectable 21.67 percent to a disastrous 8.5 percent. This shift of product mix is a subtle trap. If current-year sales follow the same mix, bankruptcy is likely.

At this point, some tough decisions must be made. The sales mix is a problem. Can Grade 1 sales be increased? Is new capital equipment required? What cost reductions can be made to improve the margins of Label 2 and especially Brand 3? Is the sales price for Brand 3 too low? If it is increased, will the resultant reductions in revenue be offset by the increased gross margin? Can Grade 1 be redesigned to cut production time (and cost)? If so, the risk of loss could be reduced.

Interest rates also fluctuate. A crash sales program resulting in increased sales of these products would necessitate investment in inventory. Capital is expensive. The increased sales must cover the cost of borrowing and storing.

Table 19-1. Gross margin analysis.

Product	Backlog	Gross Margin	Potential Gross Margin
		LAST YEAR	
Grade 1	$ 500,000	50%	$250,000
Label 2	500,000	10	50,000
Brand 3	500,000	5	25,000
	$1,500,000	21.67% (avg.)	$325,000
		THIS YEAR	
Grade 1	$ 100,000	50%	$ 50,000
Label 2	500,000	10	50,000
Brand 3	1,400,000	5	70,000
	$2,000,000	8.5% (avg.)	$170,000

The analysis of future cash payback should consider the time value of money. As you know, cash in hand today is worth more than an equal amount of cash a year from now. Analysts use tables of discount factors to determine the present value of future payments, adjusting for the time value factor to make the dollars comparable.

Example: What is the present value of $1,000 to be paid five years from today? The cost of capital is 8 percent and the discount factor, according to standard tables, is .6806. Thus the present value of $1,000 paid five years from today is $680.60 ($1,000 × .6806). Present value should be a major factor when you evaluate long-term projects or projects requiring a large initial investment and a long payback period.

MARKET SEGMENT ANALYSIS

Answers to these and other questions may require a market segment analysis to find the relationships between products and segments. In it we can use the data discussed. As we have seen, Joe's selling costs totaled $4,000 and his sales were $62,000;

thus Joe's selling costs were 6.45 percent of his sales. But Joe sells more than one product, and he covers more than one market segment. We must go further in our analysis of Joe's contribution. Time analysis might disclose that Joe's time was spent as follows:

Product	Segment A	Segment B	Segment C	Total	Distributed Sales Cost
Grade 1	5%	20%	30%	55%	$2,200
Label 2	5	20	10	35	1,400
Brand 3	3	2	5	10	400
	13%	42%	45%	100%	$4,000

Joe's expected sales, based on the time spent in each segment, would be: $8,060 (13% of $62,000) for Segment A, $26,040 (42% of $62,000) for Segment B, and $27,900 (45% of $62,000) for Segment C. Joe's sales book for the month has the following entries:

Product	Segment A	Segment B	Segment C	Total	Percent of Sales	Gross Margin
Grade 1	$ 0	$ 2,000	$ 2,000	$ 4,000	6.5%	$2,000
Label 2	3,000	10,000	1,600	14,600	23.5	1,460
Brand 3	6,000	6,000	31,400	43,400	70.0	2,175
	$9,000	$18,000	$35,000	$62,000	100.0%	$5,635
Expected sales	$8,060	$26,040	$27,900	$62,000	100.0%	

Further investigation discloses that Joe spent $2,200 (55% of $4,000) to write $4,000 of Grade 1 business (a loss of $200, since gross margin is 50 percent). Joe spent $400 (10% of $4,000) to book $43,000 of Brand 3. You'd conclude, and rightly so, that the money spent on Grade 1 sales was wasted. The analysis would also disclose that Segment B does not generate the expected sales volume.

If everything else were equal, the analyst would recommend that Joe concentrate on Label 2 in Segment B and Brand 3 in Segment C. As Joe's time and cost records show, they are accounting for 25 percent of his cost and producing nearly 67 percent of his sales. In addition, you now know that Joe is generating gross margin of $5,635 for a cost of $4,000. If his $62,000 sales were for Grade 1, the margin would be $31,000, an improvement of 450 percent. These data can be used to set sales goals for the next sales period.

We have examined a few techniques of financial analysis for sales. Many other techniques exist for production or administrative areas. Most are quite simple, although they do require recordkeeping. The time spent establishing these records is an important investment. Greater sensitivity to analytical techniques will help you become a more effective supervisor by increasing your ability to find the key decision points in your department.

20

Add Sixty Minutes to Each Day

Supervisors are busy people. You ought to know. To get everything done you need at least 25 hours a day. How can you squeeze that extra hour out of your day? Some active, energetic people add this magic hour by simply getting up earlier. Others pack themselves off to bed an hour later. The obvious message: Work longer, sleep less, and you'll automatically become more productive. Right? Working an extra hour is an easy and practical way to gain time. Unfortunately, if you work more hours and use them the same old ways, you really aren't accomplishing all you could. The real challenge is to find ways to improve your productivity.

How you use your extra hour will depend on many factors: your job, family commitments, physical endurance, preferences, life goals, and geographic location. Believe me when I say that you must really be dedicated (or slightly crazy) to find any productive use for an extra hour on a frosty morning in Minnesota with the temperature at 25° below. Even the best intentions quickly freeze. They are replaced by a new decision about the best use of your time: (1) turn off the alarm, (2) pull on another blanket, (3) roll over, and (4) hope tomorrow is warmer. The point is that you must motivate yourself to get going regardless of "conditions."

Are you using your extra "magical" hour to earn a bonanza or just to go bust? As you think about your answer, break an hour down minute by minute. How often have you said, "It'll only take a minute"? Did it? If not, did the delay annoy anyone? a lot can happen in a minute—and a lot of minutes can pass without results. An hour contains 60 minutes. That's 60 chances to get a job done, or 60 opportunities to disappoint a customer or irritate your boss.

A new maid dragged around the house doing her chores with all the vitality of a dying snail. "My, but you're slow," complained the mistress of the household. "Isn't there anything you can do quickly?"

"Yes, ma'am," replied the maid. "It only takes me a few minutes to get tired."

Is that the picture you present to your boss? It doesn't have to be. Squandering time on low-value projects leads to failure. Successful people get maximum output from a minimum investment of time.

Perhaps you can get an extra hour of output without losing any sleep. Time is your most valuable asset. Time management concepts will help you get more visible results from each minute. Here is a seven-step program that will help you decide minute by minute how to maximize one hour each day. Potential payoffs are substantial. What have you really got to lose by trying? Take one new step each day for the next week. The program looks like this:

Step 1   Decide you're in charge of your life.
Step 2   Set yourself deadlines and meet them.
Step 3   Identify your time buffers.
Step 4   Use prime time for prime projects.
Step 5   Control your attitude and behavior.
Step 6   Communicate clearly.
Step 7   Use spare time productively.

Repeat these steps each week until you've perfected them. Extra minutes will "pop" into each hour. Your output will increase and you'll be getting more satisfied looks than you ever expected.

STEP 1: TAKING CHARGE

Begin by making a conscious decision about who is in charge of your time. Every hour gives you an opportunity to save or waste minutes. And you don't have to become a clock watcher to make time work for you. Of course, not watching the clock can become a problem for some people.

Joe had a tendency to oversleep. His boss greeted him with "What's your idea of coming here late every morning?"

"It's your fault," replied Joe. "You trained me so thoroughly not to watch the clock in the office, that I don't look at it at home either."

Keep a record of how much of your time you really control. Selling is the easiest profession in which to keep score, but other professions can be scored too. How do you use minutes that suddenly become available? There are many opportunities to use normally "wasted" minutes. For example, when you're waiting for someone—whether it's in a department store, a doctor's office, the boss's anteroom for that "important" meeting, or the receptionist's desk at that major account—have some quickie projects handy. Constructively use these extra minutes to:

Work on your personality by showing genuine interest in someone.

Jot down new selling ideas or arguments.

Mentally review new report features.

Outline your next presentation.

Decide what to do when you return to your office.

Pull out and review ideas or motivational messages you've prepared on index cards.

If you aren't doing some of these things, you aren't packing your sardine can of time tightly enough.

The next question: Are you making most effective use of meetings, memos, and telephone calls? For each conversation or meeting, have you prepared a tally of points you want to or must cover? When you make your list, don't forget to cover the concerns of your customer (spouse, boss, subordinate) too. In fact, it may be helpful to list these first. The sooner the other person is satisfied, the quicker you will complete the transaction. Result: You're off to the next client or challenge that much sooner. An added benefit is that you appear more interested in others without being overly aggressive.

STEP 2: SETTING DEADLINES

If you set deadlines, then meet or beat them, you've freed up extra time. Put it to work. It is easy to set yourself goals with deadlines. It is simple to press on to achieve them. You disagree? When you arrive home tonight tell your spouse, "I have no plans for this weekend. What do you think we should do?" Don't think you're going to get off with no assignments. There's little danger that you'll wind up a captive of the "boob tube." Notice how quickly your spouse can find things for you to do—with deadlines attached too.

Your spouse will help you out by quickly creating a plan or telling you about the one he or she has been saving. Having specific plans for an evening or weekend is a morale booster for the entire family. It can also give you an incentive to get your office tasks done so they don't interfere with those family plans.

If your spouse can do it, you can too. The important step is to get started. Ask yourself a few questions to get your mental wheels moving:

1. Do I set deadlines (always, sometimes, never) for myself? For others?
2. Do I really control all my time or only some of it?
3. Do I keep a "to do" list somewhere (in my pocket, in the car, or at the office)?
4. Am I an "avoider" at work? Do I avoid making decisions or routinely arrive at meetings late? Do I duck my responsibility to train subordinates? Do I drive around the block instead of calling on Mr. Tough Customer?

5. Do I consciously avoid duplication of effort by taking a few minutes to see if anyone is already doing the assignment I just got? Do I always "start from scratch," or do I partially complete routine items before they are requested?

Your answers should help explain your success or failure at meeting project deadlines. If you're having problems, there's no time like right now to improve. Pick an objective, set a deadline, then clobber it. Build up your confidence. Work to improve your resources. Soon Mr. Tough Customer and "he can't get the big order" will change to Mr. Not So Bad and "he solved another one"! Result: You'll get more done in the same amount of time.

STEP 3: IDENTIFYING TIME BUFFERS

No time management program is complete without recognizing "time buffers." A time buffer is the built-in delay mechanism we all have. Effective time management involves channeling physical and psychic energies into recognizing realistic personal or business delays. The establishment of clear-cut goals means recognizing their importance—and the amount of time they take. To do this, you must identify the time buffers you may face on any given day. These include:

Family obligations
Delays in product development
Overcommitments
Needs to accommodate others
Negotiations
Requirement for personal flexibility
Rest and hygiene
Miscommunications
Staff training

The cost of lost time includes poor family relations, upset clients, slow job progression, untrained staff, and an unhappy boss.

Resolve time buffers to avoid their cost to you. For example, you must use time to train subordinates. Every minute you save is one you can use to train people. You will be able to delegate more of your tasks. During and after training your productivity will increase with a minimal expenditure of time. Thus, solving one time buffer can benefit you in more than one way.

STEP 4: USING PRIME TIME

Spend your prime time on *your* prime projects. Some people do their most productive work in the morning; others are at their best late at night.

In goal setting you decided what was important to you. Did you remember to identify your "best" time? Are you going to earn a prime, extra hour? Recall that you can use it in several possible ways: in the office (home or work), on the freeway (stuck in traffic), with your boss (explaining a great new idea), with a client (if he will meet you early or late), with your family, or at a library. (One excellent auditor I know starts every new assignment with a trip to the library to be sure that his technical and client knowledge is current.)

People often invest time ineffectively in striving to achieve their goals because they don't know their best (most productive) time of day. Sometimes, too, people lack information they could be using during prime time or simply lack motivation to get a job done. Effectively using prime time means finding it, then investing it to achieve what you want. Maximum usage of prime time demands that you keep your value structure clearly in focus. Use your best time to zero in on accomplishing your highest-priority goals.

STEP 5: CONTROLLING ATTITUDE AND BEHAVIOR

Control your attitude and behavior and you've saved time too. Boredom is a killer; it encourages mental and physical decay. Don't waste a single second being bored. Rip boredom out and replace it with a system of internal rewards.

As you complete a task, what happened within you? Nothing? Boredom asks, "Why continue?" The chances of doing your job productively are improved if you build a precise reward into the completion process. Complete your goal. Promise yourself a reward. Job all done? Then play that round of golf or do whatever gives you pleasure. Use your extra time to reward yourself.

Many people face a monotonous, repetitious job that threatens their self-respect. Don't waste one of your precious minutes on self-pity. Instead, manage your time so that you achieve results that please you. As you do your job, be authentic. Be the real you.

At some time, everyone is a salesman. A successful salesman follows certain expected rules. For example:

Really care about the customer.
Listen attentively.
Know what you are talking about.
Be self-assured enough to face refusal.

But just "following the rules" doesn't guarantee success. Attitude also plays a key role. You must be prompt, courteous, and considerate. Minimizing customer (spouse, boss, big customer) waiting time can help solve problems—and saves you time explaining and apologizing. This is time you save to use productively elsewhere.

STEP 6: COMMUNICATING CLEARLY

When you are introduced to a salesperson, what do you hear? Think about it for a minute. Make up a list of traits. Do you get clear communication from someone who seems trustworthy and easy to understand? Or does what you hear suggest delay, broken promises? Does your list have more positives or negatives?

It takes time to overcome negatives. Here are some things you can do about them in advance:

1. Make realistic promises on due dates (spend less time explaining delays or worrying if you can meet dates).

2. Establish a call-back system for phone calls.
3. Know your job better.
4. Establish a positive tone early in the conversation.
5. Discuss (argue) if you must, but keep the issue clearly divorced from the person.
6. Don't spend your time talking to your secretary; do your work where it counts.
7. If you can't answer a question, admit it. Write down that tough question on your note pad or index cards. Then follow up. Get the answer and call back.
8. Use words that are easily understood. Avoid double or triple meanings. Listen for misunderstandings. Clarify the points you want your prospect to understand and agree to.

STEP 7: USING SPARE TIME

Use spare time productively. Everyone has time for a few words with a friend. To go up one floor or two we will wait for an elevator, even though taking the steps would be faster and would help keep us in physical condition. Small talk about the weather must start 90 percent of "business" conversations. Weed out these practices. You'll add productive minutes to every hour.

You can find many uses for your spare time. For example:

Read and study job education materials.
Expand family relationships.
Improve physical fitness.
Outline plans for achievement.
Work on talents needing improvement.
Relax with an avocation (practice piano; build model ships).
Perfect business writing.
Practice speeches.

You've probably added a lot more ideas to your own list. Remember, you decide how your hours are used. Are you using them to achieve your personal desires? Strive for balance between work and play. Time comes wrapped in many gaily colored packages. You can use it to engage in physical or mental activity, in solitary pleasures, or in group activities.

Hours at rest can be productive too. Even your hours of sleep can be useful. I like to go to sleep thinking subconsciously about the thornier problems I face—the ones that take long, uninterrupted periods of thought to solve. I keep a pad and pencil at bedside, so that when a startling solution arrives I can immediately jot it down. The idea (good or bad) doesn't get lost.

During your waking hours keep a pen and pad or supply of index cards handy. Whenever you have an idea (related to making money, to a client or product selling point, or to a family outing) write it down. If you're driving, pull off the road. Make a note of the idea while it's fresh. You can polish it during the extra hour you saved today.

To be sure to get that extra hour, you need to get started today. Begin working on the seven steps outlined above. Or go to bed an hour earlier tonight. Sleep on it. Enjoy that extra hour. If you're working the problem, you'll earn another hour tomorrow.

If you are really inspired, you may want to follow the seven-step program *and* sleep one less hour. With two extra hours you may be able to double or triple benefits. But keep in mind that it's possible to achieve more productive work without losing sleep.

21
You Can Beat Delivery Schedules

When was the last time your department completed a production design ahead of schedule? Shipped an order in advance of contract? Submitted a cost quote before the last possible minute? It's interesting how target dates, once accepted, are acknowledged to be the earliest possible time the assigned task can be completed. Products are piled up in warehouses because "they aren't scheduled for shipment." An accountant withholds a report from management because "if I turn it in now, they'll just ask a bunch of questions or ask for the data in a different form." An engineer delays the release of drawings because "I can work on something more interesting while they think I'm working on this."

What's the result? Simply this: Subordinates who are the biggest crybabies or the best negotiators can actually set substandard schedules for themselves. They lose by performing below their abilities. And if you're their supervisor, you lose too. Are you getting what you need today? Are you able to provide what your customers (and the boss) need tomorrow? Do you know how to upgrade the performance of your department?

To meet the competition from other supervisors (and the mar-

Portions of this chapter originally appeared, in different form, in *Manage,* January 1978, a publication of The National Management Association. © 1978.

ketplace), you must set tighter schedules, and your subordinates must strive to improve performance.

THE NEED FOR QUICK RESPONSE

Recognize that with the increasing tempo of change today, developing a quick response capability is essential. And the future is likely to bring highly fluid organizations, with short, direct lines of responsibility, more extensive use of special task forces and program managers, and greater decentralization. Employees will lobby for a bigger role in the decision process. As a result, the supervisor will become more adviser and consultant—less doer and director. Tomorrow's organizations will form, then reform around the problems of the day. Yet the need for quick response will increase. Solutions will be planned, implemented, and delegated, probably from directions other than the top. Coordinating and checking the solutions will be organizationally difficult. Perhaps you've already run into this problem.

With all these developments, the need for quick response will increase. I call it QRC (quick response capability)—the ability to promptly take action in response to a stimulus. How is your own QRC? Can you give a capsule statement about the current status of anything within your area of responsibility soon after receiving a request for information or notification of a problem? For instance, a question on how basic policies affect a specific situation should be answered on the spot. QRC is aimed at rapidly generating an answer or recommendation or handing down a needed decision.

QRC depends on reliable channels of communication. These must be cross-checked to related sources of information and subject to continual review. QRC can be maintained companywide by a system of newsletters, periodicals, seminars, conferences, and other items that contribute to an understanding of the total business environment. Within your area it is validated by reliable personal contacts with interested parties within (and without) your department. At peak effectiveness QRC requires little direction from you. All you need to do is generate stress on the organization.

I'm not saying you should create an artificial work situation where everything is "due yesterday." But to get QRC when it is needed you must select the assignment, stress its importance, then demand, recognize, and reward the performance you get. If you do not get QRC output on critical events, you may have supervisory problems. These include inadequate directions from you, low department morale, stubborn feelings toward "not invented here" solutions, poor rapport with sister departments, inadequate subordinate performance, and peer pressure to not support you. Each of these severely reduces your ability to be effective. If you are dissatisfied with subordinate response, investigate. Find the cause and take corrective action.

Promptly responding to management makes good sense to you. That's one reason you earned your supervisor's job. The trick is to convince your subordinates that it is important to them too. How many poor decisions have been caused by lack of facts? Were critical ones withheld by your staff? Could a little more effort before the decision, in place of the 20-20 after-the-fact hindsight, save your subordinates considerable rework and frustration? In many cases the answer is yes. Convince your people that you need their input—promptly and completely.

As supervisor, you are part of the solution. You must respond quickly and directly to your subordinates. They expect the same quick reaction from you as you demand from them. Either way, QRC means "support." Employees who receive prompt decisions from their boss feel supported. Add encouragement and the likely result is productive relationships.

BUILDING QRC

There are several actions you can take to build QRC. The first is to encourage openness with your subordinates by being open and frank with them. Discuss day-to-day developments and decisions. If you keep subordinates informed on all events that relate to their responsibilities and interests, they will be more likely to promptly share any new information they discover.

Some supervisors are left in the dark about what's really going on at work. Their subordinates apparently work around them. Do you ever feel that your office is like your car—the courtesy lights go out every time the door is closed? You can turn the lights on from inside your car. And you can turn the lights on at work quite easily too by instituting an "open door" policy. To get quick response, you must have a positive and supportive attitude. Early commitment on your part can maximize opportunities for your subordinates to "turn on."

A second way to build QRC is to set consistent performance standards. Applying different standards to different people causes resentment and apathy. To get quick response you must do more than rely on an urgency produced by customers, "professionalism," the state of the economy, bonuses, or co-worker commitment. You can supply the greatest part of the pressure to do a good job by recognizing people who achieve consistent performance standards. Set standards high, if you will, but set them with a reasonable chance of achievement. Insist on a quick response. Settle for nothing less than everyone performing at the demanded pace. Demand that each person provide what is required as promptly as possible. Lead by example. Commit yourself to beating schedules. Stress improving your performance.

A third action is to take steps to ensure responsiveness among your subordinates. As supervisor, do you get "most favored customer treatment," or something less? Subordinates decide who they perform for. Help them decide to perform for you. Bear in mind that they take direction from alternative sources identified in Chapter 17. Included are:

Management
Peers
Sister departments
Regulatory agencies

Do your subordinates look to their peer group to set performance standards for them? Current trends in technology and management practices suggest that tomorrow's workforce will be more sophisticated, better trained, and more mobile than today's. Management procedures constantly change. Administrative processes are becoming more flexible in certain areas and more rigid in others. The highly publicized trend toward participative management will continue to increase flexibility. Employees, both as individuals and as members of organized groups, will play a more significant role in decision making. Entrenched tradition and unquestioned loyalty to one boss will gradually be replaced by loyalty to professional groups (accountants to accountants, engineers to engineers, and so on). How much peer pressure (cliques) do you find in your department today?

Your subordinates can choose to give priority to the needs and requirements of sister departments. This cooperation becomes more important as specialization of function moves each functional organization apart in education, motivation, and interests.

A company needs open communication and coordination to produce a good product. The combined efforts of sales, engineering, manufacturing, and quality control are also needed. And these functions must have good material, components, equipment, personnel, and financing. If high standards exist for manufacturing but low ones for engineering, the product might be a "kludge"—that is, the product works, but the design and technology detract from the package. By the same token, the best engineering, quality, and material will lead to unacceptable results if your firm is underfinanced and poorly staffed. How well do your subordinates work with other departments?

Government units demand quick response too. Zoning changes brought on by rapid shifts in local growth patterns and increasing state and federal regulation of employment practices have an effect on supervisory practice.

Government intervention and standardization tend to make

company policies less flexible. How this ultimate conflict will be resolved is hard to predict; however, new standards of accountability are needed today to identify the key issues in your organization. How will your firm react to these changes? Where will you fit?

Will the changes brought about by human rights commissions, city councils, OSHA, CASB, FASB, and affirmative action programs permit you to get quick response through traditional means? Probably not. Jobs will need redefinition. Personnel development programs will need reorientation.

BARRIERS TO QUICK RESPONSE

One thing you as supervisor can do to beat schedules is to eliminate existing barriers to quick response. A major barrier is the management decision-avoidance trick—like the "desk drawer decision." Of course, some decisions should be sat on. But a supervisory policy of delay, delay, delay turns most subordinates off.

Other barriers include insulation and isolation. As firms grow, so do staff departments. If staff departments inadvertently compete with line organizations, they can prevent a free flow of data within the firm. Key departments can be isolated from needed information.

Insulation can occur as many tiers of management are added. With too much management, the top echelon can lose sight of the key activities for the information/decision-making process. Thus the CEO may decide that he can't rely on subordinates. Or he may feel he's being lied to. Or perhaps he wants to "manage" the information instead of the business. In this case, intermediate supervisory approvals become meaningless. The CEO must decide everything himself. His time limits and schedule impose a bottleneck for the entire organization.

A third barrier is an "I can't do it" response from subordinates (or other departments). Define your expectations clearly so that everyone can understand. Demand a prompt, *positive* response. Find ways to get the job done.

A fourth barrier is employee turnover. You can't remember everything about every position under you. And jobs change. Every time you replace somebody, the new employee will change the job to accommodate his strengths and preferences. If you don't keep up to date with your subordinates, communication will be impaired. A loss of credibility becomes inevitable. As credibility weakens, you lose your quick response capability. So spend at least 15 minutes each day with every direct subordinate. Use this time to coach, teach, and discuss work topics, policies, and objectives. Don't forget to discuss the news "at home" too. If you show sincere interest and make yourself available, your subordinates will find it easier to confide in you—and by the way to generate QRC.

A fifth barrier, one of the toughest to break, is misuse of quick response. I've seen many highly responsible subordinates become nonresponsive because their high-priority, "must have it now" work was never used. This barrier is built by you, the supervisor. You create it every time you aren't there on the due date, when the data, design, or drawing is ready. You build the wall higher when you decide not to use a subordinate's work—without explanation.

THE QRC REVIEW

Evaluate your organization now for response speed. Do you know what its maximum response is? Find out. Your organization may be imperceptibly slowing down. Take a few minutes to review your department's QRC. How many of these telltale signs of impending delay to quick response can you identify?

1. *Increasing commitment to public service or goodwill activities.* How much of your department's output are you losing to community groups? These include Boy Scouts, baseball or hockey teams, and fund-raising events. All good causes, they

can become an outlet for the frustrated ability of your subordinates. You may be losing their creativity, enthusiasm, and dedication to your problems.

2. *Part-time jobs.* When a subordinate moonlights, invests in real estate, or begins an after-hours business, his motivation to work for you can decrease. In addition, subordinates may use company time to sell cosmetics or other products to co-workers. How much does this reduce your ability to get quick response? Initiative in employees is always good, especially if it doesn't cost you anything, but it can become a problem too.

3. *Interpersonal barriers to quick response.* Interpersonal barriers will occur as a result of jealousy, perceived mistreatment, unequal workloads, breakdown in your feedback system, and inattention to subordinate needs.

As you complete your diagnosis, you should also determine if you are getting high-quality work. Are you willing to accept the excuse that it takes longer to get higher quality? Does it really take longer to do a good job? Is there any relationship between speed and quality?

Recognize that you must compete for your subordinates' attention just as they compete for yours. Openly discuss decisions and work assignments. Ask for input from subordinates. Obtain their ideas and feelings. Change your decisions as necessary. Time lost to a timely decision change can quickly be made up by enthusiastic workers.

Bear in mind that in an increasingly complex business environment, quick response relies on the specialization and personal involvement of your subordinates. You need to expand the capabilities of your subordinates to meet tomorrow's new challenges.

Since the success of an effort often depends on how it is presented to subordinates, it is important for you to cover the areas of personal interaction and communication skills. This complements your employees' technical training to make them more effective in specific critical situations.

Start now. Practice on yourself. Make sure that you give

quick response to your superiors' requests. Give clear, concise definitions and set consistent, measurable standards. Set an example and give quick response to subordinates' requests. And whatever you do, once you get quick response, *use it*. You will be recognized for quick response capability and, better yet, you'll consistently beat delivery schedules.

PART V
Plan Your Next Step

22
Toot Your Own Horn

Although you may think you've come a long way, baby, you've just begun to climb the ladder to "success." All you've done so far is to enter the vast province called middle management. This area has limitless boundaries, and many an unlucky soul has entered never to be heard from again. If you haven't already learned it the hard way, the title "supervisor" puts you in the middle of a lot more than merely management. Getting out of this middle requires special strategies and tactics. Although this chapter is dedicated to the hardworking women supervisors out there, it contains ideas any supervisor can apply.

KEY SUPERVISORY TRAITS

As supervisor, do you know what's going on in your company? Or are you just a higher-paid peon? If you don't know the "in" management things, you may be getting fooled. Take some time to find out your situation.

Women supervisors run a special risk today. To fill quotas, they are "promoted" to foremen or first-level supervisor, but in name only. That bottom rung of the management ladder can be the toughest one of all. It seems to be greased. Learning oppor-

This chapter originally appeared, in slightly different form, in *Detroit Engineer* magazine. © 1979 Engineering Society of Detroit.

tunities come disguised as threats and problems. Subordinates never seem to do their job right. Management is always unreasonable. How you develop yourself will affect how quickly you progress to the next rung. Actions still speak louder than words. If you know how and when to take action, you know enough to be a real supervisor—a promotable one. Yet relatively few supervisors take time to identify and improve skills needed for further advancement.

There are three key ingredients to a successful supervisory career. These aren't secret. Everyone knows them:

1. Self-reliance
2. Courage
3. Need to achieve

Self-Reliance

Self-reliance means the willingness to act independently of others. One way to do this is to toot your own horn. Within the work setting, supervisors are expected to have the information and ability needed for decision making. They are expected to achieve results. But many hesitate and procrastinate because they fear something bad will happen to them. Do you? Then stop and think. What's the worst that can happen?

Many otherwise self-reliant supervisors seem unwilling to ''toot their horn'' regularly. They want recognition but are reluctant to do anything extra to get it. Do you point out your accomplishments? Why not? Are you too modest? Recognition doesn't come with the territory. No one automatically ''knows'' what you do. Survey after survey finds that supervisors and subordinates do not agree on subordinates' work, goals, and priorities. Observe the work stations in your department. How many activities and duties can you routinely identify to each colleague? Is every job being done the way you think it is? Maybe you should get your subordinates to toot for you.

Does your boss know what you do or why you do it the way

you do? If not, whose fault is that? Can you remember what you were doing last month, last week, yesterday? Did you tell your boss what you did? Then how do you expect him to remember? Why be afraid to report a good record?

Many supervisory problems—in interviewing, giving directions, disciplining, and setting objectives—are blamed on lack of training. Knowledge of technique is helpful. But for many supervisors the best training courses in the world won't help. Why? Because they lack confidence in themselves. No self-reliance.

Dolores, a very intelligent woman, lived with an inbred fear of failure. She signed up and attended classes covering every possible aspect of supervision. She diligently tried to apply the techniques taught. Unfortunately, no matter how well she knew the technical aspects of supervision, she also "knew" she couldn't succeed in applying them. After several years she failed—not for lack of training, but for lack of self-confidence.

Courage

Courage means you have the guts to take risks, to try something new, to stand up for what you believe in. It shows a willingness to learn and grow. When given an opportunity to take on a new challenge, do you argue, "It's not my job—I don't get paid to do that kind of work"? Are those the real reasons, or are you afraid to try?

Analyze your response. Compare what you think you're supposed to be doing against your job description. Then ask your boss what he thinks you're doing. Have the courage to write a new job description when differences appear. It could result in a higher grade, a better job, more pay, or all three.

Are you suppressing vocational interests because you believe you must conform to some stereotype? Are you effectively doing Job A but secretly coveting Job B? If you're convinced you are capable of doing Job B, get with it. The only missing ingredient is acting on the courage of your convictions. Set up a program, add a dash of gumption, and go. June did it. She was hired as a teller. She enjoyed the public contact. She progressed to lead teller but sought more responsibility. After several years of wanting to be trust officer she finally mustered enough courage to announce her goal—then go after it with an action plan. This took considerable effort on June's part, but she got the job and the chance to supervise several juniors.

If you are capable and can become qualified for the position of your dreams, stop dreaming. Start doing.

Need to Achieve

Need to achieve is that special quality that spells out *ambition*. Many people drop out of supervision when they find out how much extra work it entails. Are you willing to work extra hours, solve problems, dominate situations? Or do you prefer to let someone else take the dirty jobs? Often these are the ones that pave the way to business success.

Sandy had tremendous enthusiasm. With boundless energy she tackled one project after another. When a supervisory position in an accounting office was offered to her, she quickly accepted. She was the first woman supervisor of that group. So what did she find? Men working for her made more money than she did. The women in the group resented her success. They didn't provide the support Sandy expected. Her skill at preparing written reports wasn't as strong as it should be. Management didn't take her early suggestions seriously. Sandy was very nervous and stammered through oral financial reviews.

Despite these problems, Sandy refused to quit. She learned to accept these and other incidents as normal day-to-day challenges to her ability. She established objectives, then achieved them. Ambition provided the energy and motivation necessary to drive through these difficulties to final success. It took several years and more than a few tears, but today Sandy has achieved her salary goals. The women respect her for her demonstrated ability to get the job done, and she now has responsibility for two other departments. Sandy had the courage to persevere.

WEEKLY ACTIVITY REPORTS AID YOUR
CAREER GROWTH

You don't need training or a study program to improve your visibility with your boss. All you have to do is start issuing a weekly activity report. Call it "weekly events," "significant items," or "here is what I did for you today." The result is the same. You regularly put a written record of steady achievement in front of your boss. Priority items are identified. Progress on projects isn't lost. Whether the report is handwritten or typed, the objective is clear. You are getting your news to your boss in *your* words. (It's a good idea to require the same sort of report from your subordinates to improve your communication with them too.)

This report should not take the place of daily face-to-face contact, which gets the message across while it's fresh. Instead, it is intended to create a chronological file of your achievements. And it will fill the void on those occasions when your boss is not available for daily discussions. As you build up your file it can become increasingly useful. Over time it answers the question "what is he/she doing?" The file can help you develop a job description (if you currently do not have one) and can serve as justification for a salary increase or bonus. It gives you and your boss a common basis of communication. Your boss can immediately follow up on any items he doesn't understand. He may place more significance on an item than you do. The weekly report isolates these items. If you are on the wrong track, you can quickly be set right again.

When you want to change jobs, your file of these weekly reports becomes a marvelous memory-jogger for preparing a résumé. You can use it as a ready reference list of your achievements. Zero in on the employment opportunity you want by selecting those accomplishments that fit the position. For internal placement in your firm, you can easily bring to the interview with your prospective manager a recap of achievements in your current capacity.

Bear in mind that as a supervisor you are caught in the middle of management's old desire (achieving short-term profits) and management's new desire (developing people). Look out. It's a real challenge to achieve both. Whether or not you think you are a "mover" or "shaker" in your company, you do have the task of merging these opposing desires into a workable compromise.

And of course, as illustrated below, sometimes the really important actions only seem unimportant.

A hardworking, faithful supervisor was overheard complaining to a friend that she had been passed over for promotion. She stated, "I know my work thoroughly; I can do the job I didn't get. I have a fine attendance record and have kept my nose clean."

"Why didn't you get the job, then?" asked the friend.

"I guess I'm just too slow," said the disappointed supervisor.

"Too slow? Speed doesn't seem to be required on that job," observed the friend. "Anyway, lots of good people are rather slow."

"Oh, I'm not a slow worker. I'm too slow to laugh at the boss's jokes."

That's merely an excuse. Often the real problem many supervisors have is that they are too slow to report their activities.

Despite their high achievement need, some supervisors are afraid to issue a weekly report. They hide behind the question, "What format should I use?" No need to hide. Almost any format will do. In my experience, the ones commonly used closely follow the functions of the job or the department.

Marketing Department

A typical marketing department report has the following sections:

New business
Major negotiations
Major proposals
General

This report, typically written by a sales manager, identifies new customer contacts, unique sales terms and conditions, and new product ideas. The number of repeat calls is given. If higher-level management involvement may be required, it is signaled early. Expected contract or order dates are identified for large orders, making advance notice to the factory possible. Proposals for submission to potential customers are identified, including potential sales concessions and discounts. Competitors, financial risks and rewards, expected sales value, and submission date are also included.

The general category is used to identify other events considered important. Note: Lack of activity in a category is also reported. No activity may be the most significant event of the week. It could be a sign of slipping morale, overstaffing, or a dying product line.

Controller's Organization

A controller's administrative organization report may have the following sections:

Financial
Policy/systems development
General
Personnel

The report indicates the key accounting activities, including revenue earned, cash collected, and budget performance. It specifically addresses financial measures. Progress on new policies and systems is called out. New requirements or changes in old requirements are identified. Revisions to the law and their effect are reported.

The general category is used to discuss problems solved, product and new program activities, cost projections, and objectives set and undertaken with other organizations. Items such as training courses taken or offered, transfers, terminations, new hires, and vacation dates set for key people are included in the personnel section.

Design or Manufacturing Department

A typical design or manufacturing department report has the following sections:

Schedules
Standards
General

Each user states how he or she is doing by product or process against schedules and cost standards. Cost reductions are documented. Problems and solutions in process are listed. Again, a general category covers items that aren't directly related to the primary job function.

The "President's Report"

One company president requires a monthly "President's Report" which he uses for improved communication and accurate and timely information. Its purpose is to (1) provide top management with significant-events information required for critical decision making; (2) alert top management to serious existing or anticipated problems—to avoid surprises; and (3) report significant achievements that may enhance the company's image.

The president stated, "Please be reminded that this report conveys information in a rather formal, organized manner and is not a tool for requesting action or delegating (upward) responsibility for a problem. Structure your report according to these instructions:

FORMAT
- Use only the appropriate topic headings for your area of responsibility
  1. Significant bookings or negotiations
  2. Contract performance
  3. Financial commentary
  4. Administrative
  5. General

- Systems and marketing divisions and engineering, manufacturing, and quality control should normally have information in items 1–3.
- Target for no more than two pages.

CONTENT
- Cover only the most significant existing and/or expected achievements and the most serious existing and/or anticipated problems.
- Reflect the situation as of the last day of the month, even though your report is due earlier. Remember, emphasis is placed on timely data.
- Follow up problems mentioned with solutions achieved. In other words, don't mention a problem one month and never discuss how you solved it.

"You should continue to generate weekly significant-events or flash reports to communicate information or deviations from normal activity between the regular monthly reports."

The possibilities outlined above are not a complete listing. You can prepare your report in any way that makes sense to you. The point is that regular significant-events reporting is a habit. Once started, it's hard to stop. It helps you to decide your most important tasks and, as such, helps build management skills, since you specifically decide and report priority items. You report the accomplishments most important (to you). Getting agreement from your boss is a great confidence builder. In addition, your report will help stimulate greater face-to-face communication, both up and down. Have your subordinates follow the same format you decide upon. In this way you can easily "roll up" their input into your summary report.

Go ahead and do one, privately if you wish. Include only what you can remember. Recall last week. Now prepare a practice Friday report. Trial and error will help you create your own categories. Identify your major areas of accountability, then list activities or accomplishments within them. How does it look? Don't be discouraged if only one or two items come to mind, and don't be afraid to ask your subordinates for their inputs.

For this week, list events without fail every day. Build your file. Then submit the week's accomplishments to your boss. Ask for comments. Get feedback. Keep the reports coming. It won't take long to perfect your system. The result will help your future.

Tooting your horn is a lot easier if you have a good idea of what is expected of you. Do you? The general manager of a large Midwestern firm published the following list of qualities he expected in each supervisor:

Sets good example.
Communicates effectively.
Is considerate of others.
Is approachable.
Sets priorities.
Establishes clear goals.
Delegates.
Maintains a broad perspective.
Has empathy for others.

Although it is difficult to excel at all these qualities, you can try. And notice "male" is not one of the criteria.

But a word of warning is in order. Supervisors "in the middle" of the firm get to do more than the routine job. They get to handle questions such as these:

1. When will we have women at the general manager level?
2. What do you plan to do to help me cope with the increasing cost of living?
3. Is it true that "over 35" means over the hill?
4. Did you get your job because of the quota system?
5. How come there aren't more women foremen?
6. Why do older employees get fewer and smaller raises?
7. When will we get adequate public transportation to the plant?
8. Why isn't our cafeteria nonprofit?
9. When will my position be reevaluated?
10. What's the most money I can make here?

As supervisor, can you handle these questions and others just as tough?

It seems like an impossible situation, doesn't it? You may find it hard to believe, but both men and women supervisors face these same problems.

Remember, you're the supervisor. You know more than you think you do. And you do a great job too. Get out your horn and toot it a few times. It may wake up some other supervisors too.

23

When Is It Time to Do Something New?

As soon as you've developed your job to its maximum potential *for you,* it's time for a change. How do you know when that point is reached? There are a number of obvious signs. One is when all your on-the-job problems are reruns. The challenge is gone. You've already solved everything once. Another sign is when feelings of self-satisfaction and job comfort sneak into your thoughts. Are you resting on past laurels? What's your answer if the boss asks, "What have you done for me lately?"

BREAKING THE ROUTINE

If you've been in your current position for any time, you've settled into a routine. Another word for it is "rut." This rut creates a barrier to doing anything new. It also creates a negative "Look what I've got to lose" attitude. Negative thoughts can keep you stuck in old familiar habits. Here's how you can turn these negative feelings into positive actions. First, identify them as fear or lack of confidence. Second, test their validity. Third, find ways to avoid or resolve them. Now you have a set of stimulating new problems to work on.

One negative feeling that supervisors often have is "I know I

Portions of this chapter are reprinted from *The Toastmaster,* the official publication of Toastmasters International, Santa Ana, California. © 1976.

can't do it.'' Test this negative thought. It may be baloney. I know a middle-aged supervisor whose career progress has apparently been limited by the fact that she doesn't have a college degree. For 15 years she believed that she couldn't earn a college diploma. A few months ago she decided to test that negative thought. She enrolled in a college that gave credit for non-classroom learning experiences. She's doing fine so far. Whether she gets her degree or not, the point is that she is challenging a self-constructed wall that has been preventing her from improving her employment situation.

Peter Drucker, the management observer and author, says that it is not unusual for people to make the wrong career choice. He also finds that those who make the right choice are likely to get stale. Doing the same thing for 10, 15, or more years can frustrate the most positive supervisor. If you think you're in the wrong place, maybe you should change. Don't feel like an oddball if you're bored with your job.

If, as Drucker says, changing career fields is not unusual, you may be making a serious mistake by staying where you are. Bear in mind that the status quo is dangerous to your worklife. True, it's easy to stay with the old, comfortable job and its familiar problems, but a new, more demanding position may lead to greater success. If you've been in the same job for a few years, why not check? What do you have to lose? And by looking for that greener pasture, you may find that the one you have is not so bad. Or you may find ways to add new dimensions to it.

Today there are many exciting, exhilarating jobs available for men and women of all ages. These job opportunities are not always obvious. To find them, you will have to invest time in careful self-analysis and life planning, including a realistic assessment of your needs, capabilities, interests, motives, and desires.

Energy isn't a monopoly of youth. Middle and even old age is a marvelous time to develop new strengths and job-related skills and objectives. This is a time to capitalize on experience:

to think, to feel, to contemplate, to become more aware of your company and your potential to grow—in it or out of it. The perspectives gained in previous years can increase your chances for success in a second career. This could be in another department, in literature, the arts, or education, or at the firm up the street. Some of these fields are easier and less risky to enter than others.

REDISCOVERING YOUR ZIP

If supervisory duties are beginning to bore you—driving to the same old place, working the same old problems, supervising the same old people—then rediscover your zip. One way is to get involved in a volunteer program for youth. Their fresh young ideas and questions will soon boot you out of your old habits.

I met one retired supervisor who at 67 started teaching a woodworking course to underprivileged children. He claims it's the most challenging task he ever attempted. He says he's learning more about life from the kids than he can ever pass on to them. Another supervisor is a skilled scoutmaster for the Boy Scouts. As he's introduced to new supervisory techniques, he practices them on the scout council—and the scouts themselves.

How often have you seen men and women leave high-paying, important management jobs to embark on public service careers? Their motivation to change is usually for positive and compelling personal reasons. The supervisor who turns away from his job at 45 or 50 is making a deliberate choice. He has experienced one form of career satisfaction and now seeks another, perhaps more meaningful career. Often highly skilled supervisors will put their talents to work on community building projects. They seem to turn to them for new challenges, seeking greater personal fulfillment. The middle-aged or bored supervisor can benefit from trying to find solutions to the problems facing society. This benefit can come back to the job as increased management and people skills—or it can lead to a totally new career.

If you're tired of the rat race in your current position, inventory hobbies you've mastered, such as woodworking, photography, painting, or philately. Each may lead the way to something new—to a number of fields you can switch to, either as your own boss or as a nonsupervisor. The point is a hobby puts back into your workday something you like to do.

If political activity turns you on, get involved with the local party. It will enrich your life and that of your family and your community. Partisan participation in political activity is a marvelous stimulant for an apparently worn-out, frustrated supervisor. Remember, there's nothing like a good cause to make you stand up and to get your creative juices flowing again.

Sometimes health problems can lead a supervisor to make a change. If you become confined to a wheelchair or bed, make the most of it. If a heart attack or major operation temporarily stops you, productively use your recovery time. Take stock of your assets and liabilities. Take the time to really listen to music, look at art, and study literature. Use the time to think and to have new experiences. It sure beats worrying about how you're going to pay the bills or catch up when you go back to work.

Often, you can use an experience from another job or an earlier position to launch yourself into a new career. Review your résumé. It may provide you with an idea or a long-forgotten personal contact that can catapult you into a new occupation.

A word of caution. Avoid job changes for emotional reasons. Don't let a missed bonus, an undeserved rebuke, or a petty superior force you into a hasty decision. Emotional decisions are likely to be poorly thought out and financially risky. Quitting your line of work as a middle-class, middle-aged supervisor leaves you in a highly vulnerable position. Why? Because you may not have a traditional family pattern to guide you. The very rich and the very poor do. While quitting gives you a unique opportunity to create your own individual routines, it also puts you in a high risk situation. So be careful.

Any change in employment should be made to capitalize on some opportunity. And it should be your decision. Unfortunately, this is not always the case. You may lose your job for

non-performance-related reasons. Businesses fail every day. If
you are forced to face a long period without income and don't
know what to put on a job application to cover the time lost, try
"consultant." Have some business cards prepared. Advertise
yourself as a consultant. You can then honestly tell any inter-
viewer that for some period of time you attempted to make a
living in business for yourself. You can say that you found it
impossible to get sufficient business to support your family; thus
you are returning to the job market. This explanation will
usually satisfy the most persistent questioner.

A final possibility is to retire. If you make this decision, do
so by actively retiring into life rather than retreating from it.
Make up your mind that once you retire you will productively
use your time. As a retiree, you have a tremendous opportunity
to help others. The payoff may be the discovery of a new skill
in someone else. Can you get a payoff through others and be
satisfied?

Don't spend all your time seeking happiness. Instead, *find* it.
An inventory clerk made a remarkably bright discovery one day
as he tried to locate furniture missing in a dirty, dark old warehouse. In response to criticism that he was too slow, he re-
marked, "If I didn't spend so much time looking, I'd have more
time for finding." That's true for all of us, whether we are looking for furniture or career satisfaction.

Retirement can be a very satisfying time to help a spouse develop a hobby or occupation or cultivate a new field of interest.
This can be done before the children leave home or after the
nest is empty. You've been marriage partners, helping each
other over the rough times. Do the same in helping each other
find new sources of satisfaction. A single person? You too can
find retirement programs to help others through AARP chapters.

GET WITH IT

Who cares how many miles you show? You buy a "previously
owned" car on the basis of how many miles you think it has

left. At 25, 35, 45, or 60, how many miles do you have left? How much more do you plan to achieve in your lifetime? At issue here are your attitude and ambitions. Spend one hour a day for a year planning the rest of your life. Think of what you can do with 365 hours. One hour won't force you to change jobs or take time away from your present job or family. Invest that hour in your future. Set measurable goals and objectives. Decide how proficient you have to be before you can take on a new challenge. Decide how much time that will take. If you need money, find a source. Have your plan ready for execution.

Realistically face the fact that you are aging. Make a positive choice. If you make a decision you don't like, you don't have to be stuck with it. Over the hill at 40? Nonsense. Back in the 1930s people felt that life was pretty much over at 50. In the 1830s, 35 was old age. Today, people 65 and 70 are still vibrant, active people.

There are no general prescriptions for all the crises you may face. You must find your own answer to your problems. Other people have problems too. Think about them. One of the most self-destructive factors in aging is to spend all your time thinking about yourself. One woman I know does nothing but complain that she never sees anyone. She doesn't see anyone because she never invites anyone over and declines invitations to go out. She's made the decision. She has nobody to blame but herself. If she would think enough of others to do something, to get up and go, she'd enjoy a richer and fuller life.

This woman is much the same as the supervisor who sits in her corner complaining that she's left out of major decisions. To become involved she needs to get up and into the decision-making process—even if it means volunteering. Sure she'll get rebuffed, ignored, argued with, and rejected. But then, whoever said supervision was all fun and games? To get the fullest and richest supervisory experience, you must decide to stay involved.

Afraid to change? Do you think you've lost all interest? Take some interest tests. The costs aren't prohibitive. Besides finding out interests you have in common with others, you'll sharpen your test-taking skills. Don't be like the fellow who was fired and said, "It's been over 30 years since I've taken tests. I'm afraid to face them. I've forgotten what they're like."

You're more than a supervisor; you are your own salesperson. If you do get down on yourself, you've got to get up again. Without enthusiasm you won't tackle the job of selling yourself properly. You can't decide in an instant to start believing in yourself. Confidence must be built up over time.

Old isn't spelled b-a-d. Wine improves with age. Have you ever heard of New Glory, New Faithful, New Ironsides, and New Hickory? Of course you haven't. Break out of your "old" rut. Satisfaction from supervision begins at 25, 35, 45, or 60. It starts whenever you want it to. And it can last a whole career. Recommit yourself today. You may find that supervisory problems never change—but they're always challenging.

24

More About Career Paths

Help others be recognized for their ability. Assist in developing subordinates' careers. Why? Because to help yourself be promoted you must have available trained replacements for *you*.

Do you have your career path all mapped out? Do you know where you want to go next? What are you doing to get there? Will your career development program become just a long, unpleasant trip down the garden path? Will your early career expectations top out short of your goals?

Can you have a satisfying career without a career path? Sure you can. A career can be built out of a set of basic skills. In the fields of law, medicine, and the ministry, certain skills must be developed and maintained. These professions require that their members stay current in regulations, techniques, and people skills. Although professionals develop and refine their talents, there is no apparent change in their status.

For most people, though, a career path involves movement, a climbing or passing through job levels. In addition to mastering one set of skills, career growth implies learning and being able to apply new skills. Career development takes place as each new skill or job duty is mastered.

EMPLOYEE DEVELOPMENT TOOLS

As a supervisor, you are clearly the most important person in the process of career growth. Why? Because you select new employees—people who are presumably qualified for each job—and usually help develop the one to replace you. Thus to help your progress you should never select "warm bodies," people who can never be developed. You should strive to select people who want to grow. Career development starts with personnel selection, continues with job assignments, and is achieved by learning and performance on the job. The question you must always ask yourself is: "Have I selected the right people, have I started them at the right place, and am I helping them grow?"

Assuming the selection process has been properly completed, you can move on to career development programs. Again, you must answer some important questions: How many facets are there to career development? Are there growth possibilities in the same field, opportunities for development in related fields, and alternatives for entry into new fields? For career development in the same field, does a person need more than a seminar now and then or mere familiarity with current technical literature? Will this alone sustain personal growth?

About the best contribution you can make to round out a career development program is to demand that your people take on challenging assignments. Don't let them fill up all their time with routine tasks. New challenges bring new development.

One of the more popular employee development tools is a job rotation program. But before you start such a program, you must make some basic decisions about its structure:

Should employees be consulted?
Should other supervisors be involved?
Should people be recruited specifically for rotating assignments?

If you do not resolve these important issues before initiating a rotation program, you can upset many subordinates. Morale, loyalty, and work schedules may be destroyed. Without warning, one Midwestern firm announced the reassignment of 20 people as part of a new rotation program. Result: 4 quit, 5 liked the change, and 11 complained enough to be returned to their previous duties.

In considering a job rotation program, try to determine whether it will satisfy your objectives. At rotation time, several employees must simultaneously learn new jobs. They must quickly become productive. If a continuous rotation program is instituted, participants don't have an opportunity to dig in too deeply in any one area because they spend most of their time in a learning mode. This is not fair to some employees, who become frustrated because they don't have the chance to apply their knowledge and perfect it. If an employee is going to rotate, he must stop someplace. At some point rotation must end and promotion begin. For this reason, the supervisor, in a very real sense, becomes a career director and counselor. He must recognize the sacrifices his employees are making to grow and develop—the time employees must take away from their family and hobbies. On the other hand, if a subordinate decides not to grow, the supervisor must point out that he is in a limited-demand situation. His job may be eliminated or merged with another.

How can you ensure commitment to career growth? You probably can't. However, the creation of a career development team may help. The team is supervisor and subordinate. Each must profile his or her needs. Keep in mind that while an individual is trying to succeed on his present job, he could be preparing himself for a new job too.

MATCHING PEOPLE AND PROGRAMS

Be sure that you are able to discuss career objectives with your employees openly. Be sure you are really able to help direct the employee's progress in the firm. Remember, you have a bias. You must get the work done today, tomorrow, and the day after that. You may not want to develop good employees only to lose them. Thus it is very important for you to play fair.

One of the first steps in planning employee careers is to have the employee identify his development objectives. To assist in the selection process, you may want to create a central file of current job descriptions for each position in your department or company. Each description should indicate job duties, hours of work required in an average week, and travel requirements. You could include every position from the president on down. The file should be made available to all employees so they can zero in on the jobs that interest them. Next, have each employee complete a career development objectives form, such as that shown in Figure 24-1. (The questions may need modification to fit your particular needs.) Answering the questions forces the employee to recognize needs and state objectives—and in a format that he can bring to you as a basis for discussion.

You'll also find out if somebody has made a mistake. With a career plan, the employee can avoid problem jobs. There is no reason for needlessly spending time in jobs that don't fit. Recognize that if an employee didn't understand the job he was hired into, if he was oversold or overqualified, he can become embittered and lose any opportunity to be promoted.

Some people don't want to advance. They want to stay in the same geographic location or the same department. They may want to avoid traveling or working long hours. Respect their decision, but help them realize that they may be severely limiting their ability to progress with your firm.

Subordinates, when asked for their career targets, may be evasive. They may have personal problems they want to keep hidden. They may have health problems. There could be many reasons an employee will not be able to give you a definite career plan. So don't force it on him today. Give him new chances again and again. Although it's his career, shape it were you can.

Acceptance of trainees by other career people can be unpredictable. Different rates of pay can cause morale problems. You may hear, "Here I'm training those people and they are getting paid more than I am." This can cost you something too. Therefore, remember that your program must be successfully sold to gain acceptance. Concentrate on selling benefits to all parties.

Figure 24-1. Employee career development objectives.

Employee _____

Date _____

1. To master my present job, I must:

   _____

   _____

2. My next two-year career objectives:

   First Year _____

   Second Year_____

3. Specific positions currently in existence that I feel I am ready to handle:

Position	Now	A Year from Now	In 2 Years
_____	___	_____	_____
_____	___	_____	_____

4. Steps I have taken to improve or prepare myself to qualify for those positions (seminars, education, reading, volunteer work, etc.):

   _____

   _____

5. My major strengths and areas for improvement (as they relate to achieving my career objectives):

Strengths	Areas for Improvement	Plans for Improvement
_____	_____	_____
_____	_____	_____

6. Areas in which I need help to accelerate my development:

   _____

   _____

If you have no career planning program today, you may want to develop one and try it out on a few volunteers. See who is willing to take the risk of putting ideas and objectives in writing. Some may fear that once their desires are out in the open, they will be in danger. Further, bear in mind that some people can't answer. They don't know what they want. Help make them aware of what they could be doing. Give them the coaching and encouragement they need to understand that they, to a great degree, control their own lives and careers. What you really are trying to find out is what the employee wants, what the employer wants, and whether the two are compatible.

The goals of your career development program may be:

1. To improve effectiveness on the current job.
2. To get the employee to recognize his individual responsibility.
3. To get management to recognize its obligation to provide an environment in which development can take place.
4. To ensure that most career development takes place on the job, at work.
5. To help perpetuate the business and make it grow.

Achievement of these goals depends on the proper utilization of human resources. They are vital to having a marketable product delivered on time at a profit.

Set goals for achievement on the job and have a system to measure and reward career development activities. Rewards may be in salary differentials, special recognition, or protection from economic uncertainties. If an employee is working diligently to improve on-the-job performance, he or she should be protected from layoff as long as possible. The sacrifices the employee is making for the company are increasing this value for the future.

THE FIRST YEAR—POTENTIALS AND EXPECTATIONS

The first year on the job is critical for many employees. This is demonstrated by the high turnover rate in entry-level jobs. As supervisor, you've tried to reduce that first-year turnover rate by selecting employees carefully and by openly discussing each employee's objectives in terms of career growth. The next step is training. Some companies give only minimum training in the first year. They put their employees right on the job, to sink or swim. Only those who make it through the first year get any substantial training. The economics of this approach seem unassailable. Why invest training dollars if a person is going to fail anyway? Other companies spend a considerable amount on first-year training in order to develop high productivity early. You have to pick the system that works best for you.

One of the problems you face is that you must rely on a few key people to keep the department running smoothly. Your promotion, salary, and other policies must be geared to keeping and developing these key people. You must be familiar with the backgrounds of these people and keep abreast of their progress toward career goals. You must know if their goals change. Otherwise, you may suddenly lose a key employee because you were directing him along a path he didn't want to be on anymore.

In order to test this, prepare a set of supervisory guidelines for your key employees. (See Figure 24-2.) In doing so, you put yourself on the line and, in effect, tell the employee what you think his target should be within the company. You also give the employee an opportunity to discuss in some detail what he must do to meet your expectations. The employee learns where and when he can expect to grow and what he must do to get there.

At this point, recognize that some individualists will refuse to plan their careers. These people may be productive and successful. However, without specific objectives and yardsticks, they may take longer to reach their potential, and they are not likely to do as well as the employee who particpates in regular career planning sessions and follows a plan for growth.

Job Competition Produces Losers Too

If three people compete for one job, two are going to lose. You'll have to decide what to do with the losers. Career devel-

Figure 24-2. Supervisory career development guidelines.

Employee _____

Date _____

Supervisory Career Development Guidelines

With your experience and educational background you can reasonably expect to set your career target within the _____ Division to be (exempt/nonexempt) grade _____, in the (1-2-3-top) quartile. This assumes you are self-motivated to maintain a maximum work effort and consistently improve productivity. In my judgment, your potential target should be reached by __(date)__. Over time this translates into a salary of $ (amount). If you are unable to achieve this goal by __(date)__, you should definitely reconsider your career objectives and performance against them.

The ranges and salaries are stated in today's dollars according to today's salary and grade structure. The minimum salary for grade _____ is $ (amount). The maximum is $ (amount). If you desire to progress beyond these targets, it is my opinion that you must take the actions below. Both the personnel manager and I are always available to you for career counseling.

Supervisor _____

Action Program	Completion Date	Expected Impact	
		May Raise Performance Rating	*May Raise Job Grade*
_____	_____	_____	_____
_____	_____	_____	_____
_____	_____	_____	_____
_____	_____	_____	_____
_____	_____	_____	_____
_____	_____	_____	_____
_____	_____	_____	_____

Figure 24-3. Employee career development record.

Employee Name _____

Department _____

Date _____

Current job title: _____

Description of work: _____

_____

_____

Training needed on current job: _____

_____

_____

Training planned for this year: _____

_____

_____

Previous education and training: _____

_____

_____

Work experience: _____

_____

_____

Languages: _____

Strengths: _____

Weaknesses: _____

Plans for development: _____

_____

_____

opment is not a one-shot deal. You have to chart alternative courses for the people who don't win the jobs they want. This often requires a deep understanding of people's abilities, ambitions, goals, and needs.

At some time, you will be confronted with the question, "Why did Joe get promoted and not me?" You've got to respond openly and frankly. Don't give employees a story like, "You don't have a college degree." Sooner or later they're going to find someone getting promoted without a college degree. If the real reason is attitude, say so. State the employee's strengths and weaknesses on a career development record, such as that shown in Figure 24-3. Summarize the employee's progress and point out what he's going to work on next. This review should help the employee understand why he is being rated the way he is and how he can continue to develop, with or without a promotion or job change.

Dual Ladders

For many years, it has been widely accepted that to have a successful career a person must be promoted to a management position. This is not necessarily the case. Look at Figure 24-4, which shows two development ladders that start from a single ladder at the entry level and progress through the learning levels. At the decision level, the employee must decide whether he should continue up the technical ladder or go to management.

This is one answer to the question, "What's at the end of the path?" If the employee has good technical competence, he should be able to climb the technical ladder, progress in pay, and gain the various trappings of prestige just as if he were a manager. Technical specialists predominate in the fields of law and medicine. There is certainly nothing wrong with staying on the technical ladder. Unfortunately, the mystique of management is so strong that many people try to succeed as managers even though they have no desire to manage.

By the time he reaches the top, the senior specialist on the technical side may be equal in status to the senior manager on

Figure 24-4. Development ladders.

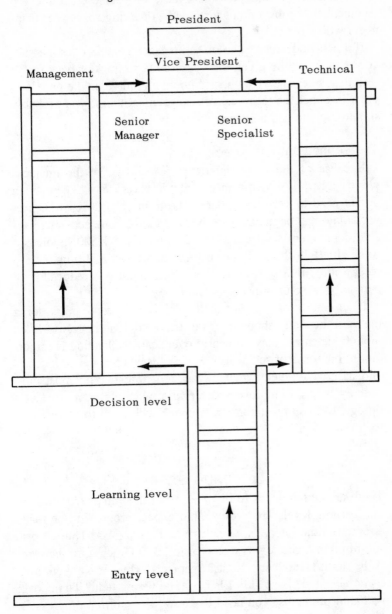

the management side. This assumes, of course, that the top technical staff jobs are not just used as parking spaces for managers who have failed.

If a person decides to go on to management and does not succeed, he should be given the opportunity to transfer back to the technical side, and vice versa. Should an individual be unable to grow in either the technical or management areas, you probably should recommend a change in career fields.

The Topped-out Employee

Because of the increased tempo of change in the business world, jobs are growing in complexity every day. There is an urgent need to keep up to date. The training and experience of yesterday may be inadequate today. In 1968, one accounts payable department with a staff of 20 processed 1,500 invoices a week. In 1978 the same department processed 3,300 invoices a week, but with a staff of 12. The department was reduced by 8 people because of improved technology.

If an employee has been with you for 25 years and is doing the best he can, shouldn't you leave him alone? No. Even though his career may be nearly over, career planning is important to his sense of self-worth. Keep older employees productive and assured of their value to the department. You must continually help all employees determine which skills need developing. And you must constantly check with them to be sure that they don't feel left behind.

JOB PROGRESSION

There are certain steps to be taken from the entry level through the learning levels, and you should expect progress to be made at certain time intervals, as shown in Figure 24-5. Thus, a person hired into Grade 4 is expected to go to Grade 6 in one year. If he hasn't, you should ask yourself why. Have you miscommunicated? Is he slow? Is he in the wrong field? To uncover potential problems, you need to know what normal progress is. You've got to chart it and be ready to measure your people

Figure 24-5. Normal progression within job levels.

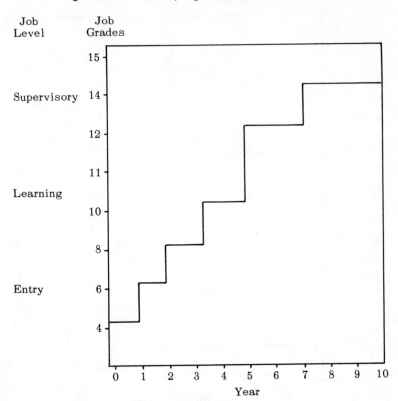

against your standard. "Normal" progress will vary from industry to industry, from field to field, and from department to department. You must know what it is for *your* department.

Figure 24-6 indicates what can happen where you've generated a good program, sold it to your employees, and gained their commitment. You know the normal progression. The employee actually progresses faster than normal. You are pleased. He is not. He is not progressing as fast as he wants to. So no matter how things seem to be going for you as supervisor, remember you must know how they are going for the subordinate too. High expectations can lead both to high motivation and to disappointment.

Figure 24-6. Measuring actual and expected job progression.

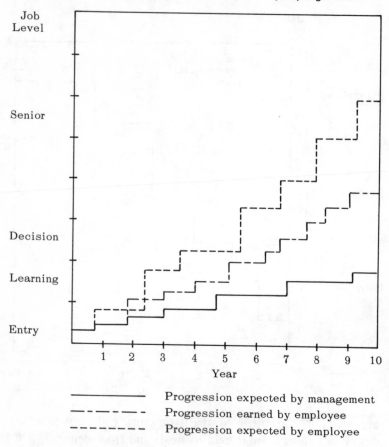

Are you going to involve yourself? When you try to solve problems, you learn new skills and in the process strengthen your own capabilities. In this way you can develop, even in a stagnant business. The incentive for career development is the fact that change is taking place all the time. This constant change is why you too need a career path and why you must keep growing.

25

Who's Planning Your Survival?

Can a supervisor survive in one company easier than in another? Of course he can; it's always easier to survive in the other guy's company.

Sometimes it seems that a supervisor has about as much protection as a ship without waterproof bulkheads. If even a small hole is gouged in its side, if the pumps don't work and the crew is unable to seal the hole, the ship will gradually fill with water. The captain and his mate can stand on the deck reciting from an emergency plan until the ship sinks. Or they can yell, "This is an emergency!", drop the plan, and head for the lifeboats. Heading for the lifeboats is the last phase of this survival plan.

Survival takes luck, hard work, and a plan. The real starting point is "the plan." Inadequate survival planning, with resultant poor staff support, causes countless supervisors to sink a little lower in the water too. To be effective, a supervisory survival plan need not be formal or set in concrete. But it must contain well-conceived, long-range objectives that are consistently applied through strategies, then upgraded by experience, training, and opportunity. They must result in short-range actions that serve as easy-to-apply course corrections whenever a crisis arises.

STAYING AFLOAT

Does this suggest that one plan, imperfect though it is, may be your only course to follow? Yes, it does. Applied to supervisory planning, the approach is completely valid—with one additional requirement. The plan must be *flexible*, subject to periodic review and improvement. You must be ready to capitalize on opportunities, to take shortcuts, and to measure achievement against objectives. The plan must include built-in evaluation points so changes can be promptly made when required.

Without such a plan, a supervisory career becomes no more than the cumulative product of the circumstances of the moment. Control is lost. Effort is wasted. The result is dissatisfaction, frustration, or worse. On a national level we've blindly reacted to the energy, paper, and metals crises without taking any steps to solve or even identify the what-can-happen-next problem. A similar series of personal crises could happen to you: new boss, a merger, illness, divorce. With a plan, you can still climb the ladder to success (a form of survival) in spite of these potent career stoppers.

Supervisory survival involves deciding in advance what, why, when, where, how, and who will achieve which objectives. Designing implementation strategies requires objectivity. You must try as hard as possible to keep your ego out of the process. The final step—quantifying and putting dollar price tags on the individual parts of the plan—is also a challenge.

Planning is an art; it will never be an exact science. It requires a lot of guessing about the future. As a result, the data and objectives developed will present only a crude picture of what may happen. Don't be overly concerned about that. You will never have all the facts—but neither will anyone else. In planning for the future, you would *like* to be sure, but certainty is unlikely. By working out a plan you come closer to predicting the future than if you abandoned planning altogether. And if you make no plans, you may have little time to react to hostile turns of events. A wrong response can sometimes put you out of a job.

MINIMIZING GUESSWORK

Supervisors don't have to plan in a vacuum. General management gives direction to supervisor planning efforts when it issues policy statements and outlines specific objectives regarding income, strategies, growth rates, and other items. Line and staff supervisors must know what these targets are. A clear, specific statement of direction and action is the cardinal contribution of corporate management to the supervisory planning process. Be sure you understand them. Once management decides upon and communicates its course of action, supervisory planning for achievement begins.

There are background materials available that can minimize your "guess factor" and help you quantify the need for change. The large volume of statistical data available from government publications, market research, sales forecasts, business periodicals, and industrial studies can be useful as a broad framework for your plans. Selecting appropriate sources of information is the cornerstone of your planning system. These sources include:

Management directives	Personnel department
Trade publications	Purchasing section
Peer groups	Subordinates
Marketing information	Customer relations
Financial requirements	Government publications
Products	EEOC releases
Research and development	Professional associations
Consultants	Public libraries
Procedures and policies	Competitors
Staff functions and meetings	Friends and acquaintances

You can also project trends by asking yourself these questions:

1. Is my workload increasing slower or faster than that of other departments? (Keep historical records on your workload and compare notes with other supervisors. Talk to marketing people.)

2. At what rate is my "served market" growing or shrinking? (Your served market may be management, a warehouse for finished product, or volume of invoices. Carefully monitor it.)

3. Is the rate of change increasing or decreasing? (Any change in rate signals a change in the demand for your service or product.)

4. Is there a major shift in work techniques, mechanization, or other factors? (Technology and productivity improvements are a fact of life. Be a leader in making change—don't just let it happen to you.)

5. Do I have a forecast of the effect of the new sales blitz? (A sales campaign affects everyone. Be prepared for results.)

6. How will my department be involved in future or potential products and customers? (Is your department or section in the mainstream or slipping into the backwaters? Stay in the mainstream.)

7. What does management expect from my department? Is it changing? (Supervisory survival and growth require living up to and exceeding management expectations. Talk to management. Listen. Provide the product or service required. And be positive about it.)

The scientific method of problem solving suggests an outline to follow in your planning that works whether fast or slow reaction is needed. The steps are as follows:

1. Formulate an objective (or a hypothesis to prove).
2. Collect data about what is required to achieve the objective.
3. Weigh the data to determine their value and application to achievement of the objective.
4. Frame several solutions on the basis of the data and your expectations, desires, or requirements.
5. Select the solution that appears best and most logical to accomplishing your objective.
6. Decide on an action plan, capitalizing on the solutions

selected. You may require a backup plan in case your primary plan fails.

7. Outline your plan, noting critical items, times, dates.
8. Start working the plan.
9. Carefully monitor the critical items in light of changing conditions.
10. Change the plan—and your objectives—only if a return to the original plan is not feasible.

How can following that outline help you solve your supervisory problems? Very easily. A supervisor already has many routine planning-related responsibilities. For example: (1) collecting and integrating data, judgments, projections, and objectives: (2) establishing manload and cost rates for departmental budgets and financial performance measurements; (3) obtaining approval for and then measuring accomplishment of departmental goals; (4) correlating planning efforts with the overall company plan; (5) maintaining an adequately trained workforce; and (6) rewarding subordinates.

But bear in mind that plans come in a variety of shapes and sizes. They may have several operating speeds. Some plans have to be quickly made and executed. The complete life cycle of the original hula hoop was about four months. Yet before industry could stop producing or create alternative products, it made more hula hoops than there were children in the United States. The lesson is that without an appropriate plan you can produce too much of a good thing. Carefully size the demand for your services. Supplying more than is needed can be as big a problem as supplying too little.

In the scientific planning process the supervisor should be a solution seeker. He should be a realist and have a positive approach to building solutions. The supervisor should be rational and curious and act as a catalytic agent. He should have integrity, the ability to work creatively, a practical sense of efficiency, and a realistic sense of proportion. The supervisor should have confidence in himself, and his judgment should not be clouded by emotions. He should be willing to expect and admit to a certain amount of errors.

What doesn't the supervisor do? He doesn't make up a plan without the participation of his staff. Subordinate involvement and support are critical to supervisory survival. Supervisors certainly are expected to use their experience as a basis for planning, but not at the risk of overlooking a key input. You've heard of the company that calculated its revenue plan by taking a forecast from marketing and dividing by three; then multipling by three the production cost estimates; next doubling the time estimated for further research and development; then adding a few psychological factors; and finally issuing a beautiful but totally unrealistic and unsupportable plan. No one works to achieve it—not even the inventor.

Supervisors must manage change. Change is normal, but if you switch goals repeatedly, because of subordinate or superior turnover, indecisiveness, or any of a hundred other reasons, confusion will result. There are practical limits to the number of variables that any mind can effectively handle—and to people's ability to adapt to them. Limit the number of variables in your plans.

The changing environment makes survival plans necessary. Every change requires a reaction. A plan for change mentally prepares you for the unexpected and tends to increase your level of accomplishment—both because it contributes to recognition of efficient supervision and because it makes subordinates feel uncomfortable resting on their laurels.

Your survival plan provides a critical baseline by allowing you to *measure your performance*. Yet many supervisors won't plan. They see measuring performance as a personal threat. Fear of measurement, or discouragement over slow progress, becomes a reason for strong resistance to planning. Don't let that stop you. If you create a plan to measure performance and things don't work out, at least you will find out early enough to do something about it. You can change jobs or departments, or look for another firm.

CONTINGENCIES

Allowing for contingencies must be an integral part of planning. The ban on cyclamates a few years ago involved many of the nation's supervisors and managers. When one firm received notice of the ban, management realized it was in trouble. The company's plan made no allowance for a replacement for the cyclamate base used in several of its products. But the existing plan was still a factor in the final solution. The company made a remarkable recovery by innovating around the routine plan. Through a crash project, the company found a replacement in 25 to 30 uninterrupted hours of research. Many production-related problems were solved, inventory and related losses were held to a minimum, and some inventory was relabeled to meet government specifications. Replacement products were ready for final consumer research and testing in record time. This firm was able to resolve its problems as they occurred. Its supervisors were mentally prepared to create and execute a plan. The experience again demonstrates that planning efforts must be creative, dynamic, and flexible, week in and week out.

Bear in mind that if your company is decentralized, the ambition of one division or department can affect (erode) the performance of the corporation as a whole. It is natural to expect a division head to devote his greatest efforts to areas in which he is most involved. You must weigh this against your goals. In many organizations, supervisors are less interested in improvement than they are in merely surviving by satisfying their boss with an acceptable performance level.

FINAL TOUCHES

Survival planning depends on clear and effective communication. Hurt feelings, lack of cooperation, useless estimates, and foot dragging can be minimized with a tactful human relations job by the supervisor. Human relations skills are more important than a financial, engineering, marketing, or production background.

An effective results reporting system complements planning

activities. Insist that reports to you be designed to:

Focus on the future.
Call attention to trends.
Compare performance with standards or plans.
Communicate simply and clearly.

The academic world continues to discover, the business press continues to interpret, the executive continues to look at tomorrow, and the supervisor is left alone to cope with today. Today is full of snags and hazards. When you, as supervisor, make your plans, discuss them with your staff. Listen and react. Try to achieve a coordinated team effort. The flexible plan so created, based on a consensus of expectations, will integrate the efforts of all functions toward fulfillment of corporate goals. Result: Your career has watertight compartments, pumps, repair materials, and the support of a motivated crew. When disaster strikes, the successful supervisor not only survives to plan again but sails on to a bigger job as well.

As you cruise off into the sea of tomorrow, consider that by perfecting the principles of supervision you will create the best possible survival plan. By developing a personal style, really listening and then acting on what needs action, thoughtfully and completely evaluating subordinates, diligently applying productive work habits (really *leading* by example), and establishing a career goal, you have established a survival plan. It's called outstanding supervisory performance.

My congratulations again. You are a supervisor. Now get to work on it.

Index

DATE DUE